THE ART OF
DELEGATION

THE ART OF
DELEGATION

How to

EFFECTIVELY
LET GO

with 20-34 Employees

LAURIE L. TAYLOR

TABLE OF CONTENTS

Staying ahead of your growth curve is critical to gain traction in a growing company. One of the rules that govern the 7 Stages of Growth says:

"What you don't get done in any stage of growth doesn't go away."

Getting focused on the right things at the right time is a formula for success. If you are the owner of a Stage 3 company, I invite you to also read my first two books to help you identify other issues from previous stages of growth. You can find them on Amazon.

Survive and Thrive:
How to Unlock Profits in a Startup with 1-10 Employees

Sales Ramp Up:
How to Kick Start Performance and Adapt to
Chaos with 11-19 Employees

INTRODUCTION

Hang on to your sanity, your world just shifted.

You've grown to a Stage 3 company with 20 – 34 employees.

A strange phenomenon occurs with the addition of employee #20. I liken it to when your pre-teen, who used to think you walked on water, now thinks you're dumb and dumber.

You are just a few months shy of a staff revolution. You've felt the change. Your employees are harder to manage, they push back more often and their attitude hits you in the face when you least expect it. You seem to be at odds with them on a daily basis.

Here's a hint. Don't point the finger at them; look at yourself. You have to make some changes, quickly.

In Stage 1 and Stage 2, a company is CEO-centric. When you move into Stage 3, it becomes Enterprise-centric, which means it's too big for you to continue wearing all the hats. It's time to start passing those hats around to the incredibly talented people you have hired. You have also just come through a Wind Tunnel; a chaos zone that requires letting go of outdated methodologies and adapting new ones. That's a lot for any CEO to deal with.

Stage 3 has the highest incidence of CEO-burnout than any other stage of growth. To save yourself and your company, you have to start managing, delegating and team building like there's no tomorrow.

Four out of your top five challenges center on people issues. If I've heard it once, I've heard it a thousand times from business owners: "If only I didn't have to deal with employees."

> Stage 3 has the highest incidence of CEO-burnout than any other stage of growth.

As a company moves into this critical third stage of growth, it's no wonder that many CEOs lose some of the enthusiasm and passion that was their lifeline up to now. Now you have to start relying on your people by trusting, believing in, managing, training, teaching, coaching, rewarding, caring and communicating with each and every person in your company—daily.

Want to know how to avoid a staff revolution? One word: Communication. Lots of it. Now. Today. Tomorrow. Next week. Next month.

In my workshops, I suggest managers should meet with their direct reports once a week for at least 30 minutes. Recently, a participant quickly did the math for nine direct reports and said, "You want me to spend 4 ½ hours a week talking to my employees? Who has that kind of time?"

There's your staff revolution.

Your employees are just as excited about the success of your company as you are. Give them a chance to succeed. Evaluate your leadership style and ask yourself: Is my leadership style hindering the success of this company? If you tend to micro-manage or take the command and control approach to leadership, you're in trouble.

Stage 3 demands that you let go and bring your key people into the fold. Stage 3 leaders need to be people-focused, rather than profit-focused. Focusing on people will help to improve profitability and you'll be able to put critical processes in place. Tapping into the intelligence of every single person in your company allows you to take the first step toward building a company that doesn't revolve around you.

With 20 – 34 employees, a leader is challenged with staff buy-in, a widening leadership/staff communication gap, weaknesses in the business design and fuzzy core values. The family-type atmosphere of the earlier stages changes ever so slightly, which causes people to resist change.

Your employees are just as excited about the success of your company as you are.

Many companies never make it past Stage 3; the revolving door starts early. When you hire smart, capable people who aren't allowed to be smart or capable, they will leave. Wouldn't you?

As companies grow, the complexity level of the organization increases. That complexity level doesn't increase because of revenues, profits or equity growth. Complexity increases because of the one factor in a company that is the hardest to control: people!

James Fischer, author of the book, *Navigating the Growth Curve*, discovered that as companies add more people to the equation, the dynamics change. Fischer developed the 7 Stages of Growth to address entrepreneurial companies struggling to manage growth, from 1 – 500 employees. I worked with him for five years as a managing partner at Origin Institute.

Through my current company, FlashPoint!, I have spoken to thousands of CEOs regarding the unique 7 Stages of Growth business model. The information resonates with CEOs immediately.

> ## Complexity increases because of the one factor in a company that is the hardest to control: people!

At a presentation to over a hundred CEOs, a seasoned CEO, now running his twelfth company, said:

> *"After eighteen years of doing turnarounds and twelve years of investment banking, I finally found a system that prescribes the ideal management styles and focus for different sized companies. I am on the board of a private company and will be applying the Stages of Growth techniques when advising this company."*

This reaction is typical from a CEO who has been around the block, who understands the challenges of growing a successful company and who understands that simply reading the next how-to, book of the month isn't a formula for building a successful company.

The 7 Stages of Growth gets CEO's attention because the concepts allow a business owner to do three things.

1. Predict how growth will impact them.
2. Get them focused on the right things at the right time.
3. Adapt to necessary changes as the company grows.

This model allows you to look at the past, the present and the future in order to better understand what hidden agents are impacting your ability to grow. Once you identify those hidden agents, and put a name to the underlying issues, you can solve them and move on.

The 7 Stages of Growth provides every single employee the ability to understand the challenges a company faces as it grows. Each challenge can be discussed in terms everyone understands, thereby taking the mystery out of running a company.

The impact of creating a "language of growth" starts with understanding that language doesn't *describe* a person's experience, it *defines* their experience. Change the language and you change the experience.

> *"Running a successful company isn't easy. Laurie introduced our company to the 7 Stages of Growth and recently our management team went through the Stages of Growth X-Ray process. We were able to better understand that what we were experiencing was typical for our stage of growth and identify clear objectives that are critical in order to reduce our chaos. The process also allowed us to become aligned behind those specific objectives. As we move into a new stage of growth, I feel hopeful that we've gained much needed traction and most importantly, I believe our team is better prepared for what's to come."*
>
> -Carla Schlosser, CEO, Schlosser Signs

I know business owners struggle to focus on the constant barrage of issues that come their way every day. A fast-growing enterprise can quickly grow beyond the owner's ability to manage everything.

This book addresses critical areas of focus for a Stage 3 Company. You may not define growth by the addition of employees. You may think growth means creating a business with a solid income for as long as you want it. Or, you may just be starting to consider the amazing possibilities your company has to offer and are looking for ways to manage it as you grow.

Because Fischer's model is built on the premise that additional people adds complexity, you have to make it a high priority to build the kind of environment that attracts, fosters and retains talented employees. To that end, building a profitable company depends on your ability to manage people.

One of the rules that govern the 7 Stages of Growth is: What you don't get done in any stage of growth doesn't go away. As a Stage 3 company, you may find value in reading my first two books, *Survive and Thrive: How to Unlock Profits in a Startup with 1 – 10 Employees* and *Sales Ramp Up: How to Kick Start Performance and Adapt to Chaos with 11 – 19 Employees.* Those books address issues you may have missed or ignored in earlier stages of business growth.

> Building a profitable company depends on your ability to manage people.

Stage 3 owners face one of the biggest challenges of running a successful company: Letting go. With 20 – 34 employees, you can no longer manage everything on a daily basis. I'll explain how you can prepare for the transition, learn how to embrace managing people and understand the art of delegation.

The end result is yours to determine. You have taken the first step in developing a strong foundation by considering the research-proven concepts that support the 7 Stages of Growth enterprise development model. As your company continues to add employees, I hope you return to my websites often to learn more about the challenges of each of the 7 Stages of Growth.

I wish you success in growing your business!

Your Success. My passion.

Laurie Taylor, President
FlashPoint! LLC

www.igniteyourbiz.com

www.growthcurvespecialists.com

www.destination-greatness.com

www.bizchallenges.com

Chapter 1:
What a Stage 3
Company Looks Like

A Stage 3 company has 20 – 34 employees. What worked yesterday, with less people, will no longer work today. In Stage 3, there are too many employees to manage by yourself. Your goal needs to be "let go to let it grow." How do you do that? How do you trust that anyone, other than you, will care as much, worry as much, and handle all the details as well as you have?

Stage 3 is called Delegation for good reason. The art of delegation involves transferring some of your functions onto others so they can act on your behalf. Delegating is problematic for many small business owners because it involves relinquishing some control. However, it is a vital skill for small business success. No one can be good at everything. Running a small business requires so many different tasks and skills that a division of labor is necessary for growth.

One of the biggest barriers to delegation is the false perception that you don't have enough time to adequately explain the task, or teach the skills necessary to complete the task. The tendency is to continue doing everything yourself. Even though you may be faster and know more today, this practice is not sustainable. With a growing staff, more customers, increasing revenues and expenses, your ability to delegate is your ticket to sanity.

Ask yourself:

- How well am I adapting to growth?
- How are my leadership skills?
- Am I able to let go of critical aspects of the company to capable people?
- Am I watching the key indicators of success every day?
- Am I setting clear expectations and managing to those expectations?
- Am I hiring the right people? How will I know?

In a Stage 3, Enterprise-focused company, the leader must pass off a certain amount of authority and responsibility. Too many business owners ignore what they have to do to allow their company to grow beyond the span of their control.

Here are three things you can do to help you move the company from being CEO-centric to Enterprise-centric.

1. **Hire quality people that know more than you.** You don't have to have all the answers. If you are the expert in selling your service or product, capture the essence of why you are so successful.

Then hire experienced sales people and teach them your process while learning from them how to improve those processes. Your success will depend upon recognizing and hiring good talent, being a good manager and getting out of their way.

2. **Recognize the value your employees bring to the company**. Take the timc to engage them in the thinking process. Don't assume they "just want to do their job" or they "don't understand the customer." Talk about strategy daily. Talk about their issues. Ask questions that encourage their insight. Let them know you want to hear from them. Be transparent and authentic in interactions with your direct reports.

3. **Embrace processes in order to allow more freedom**. The sooner business owners embrace the idea of creating processes that allow people to succeed, the sooner they can step away from the day-to-day and focus on the right things at the right time. Give people the ability to take charge of certain aspects of the company without having to check in with you on every little issue.

If you don't adapt to new changes and let go, you may suffer the trauma of leadership inefficiency and experience "entrepreneurial burnout."

In Stage 3, the owner must give the authority to make decisions and the responsibility of the work to the supervisors, while also managing, orchestrating, and empowering them. Your primary goal is to transition from an Entrepreneur to an Operational Manager. To do this, shift your focus to teaching others different aspects of running your company. Start by building trust among your supervisory staff and distribute key activities critical to the growth of your company.

As the CEO of a Stage 3 company, 10% of your time should be devoted to fine-tuning the vision of the company, 30% should be spent as the technician or the specialist and 60% should be spent managing people. This percentage blend is referred to as the Three Faces of a Leader. Now is the time to examine your own leadership strengths and weaknesses.

In his book, *No Man's Land*, Doug Tatum recognizes a "pivotal stage in a business's life cycle, the adolescent stage in which a rapidly growing firm is too big to be small, but too small to be big." He identifies this phase as when the company exceeds 20 employees and refers to it as No Man's Land. If a company makes it through No Man's Land, it can become a business breakout. Within these pages, I'll provide business owners with the specific solutions they need to implement to break through the No Man's Land and build a strong and vibrant company.

Part of Fischer's research for the 7 Stages of Growth uncovered what he refers to as the Non-Negotiable Leadership Rules. These are the rules a leader has to adhere to in order to manage through the unseen issues that can derail a company's growth trajectory and help you navigate the pitfalls common in No Man's Land.

REQUIRED LEADERSHIP SKILLS

The statement, "Your people ARE your business" has never been more relevant. Your focus has to shift to addressing employee issues as you learn how to delegate, teach, guide, mentor and engage your team to help you build the company. Identifying key individuals who can take on more and more responsibility requires a CEO who recognizes the value of surrounding themselves with capable people.

Essential skills for growth include:

- Ability and desire to manage people
- Awareness to assign enough supervisors
- Willingness to delegate authority and train for that authority
- Manage, orchestrate and empower the supervisors
- Address cost issues
- Put critical processes in place

I promise, if you take the time to study the 5 Challenges outlined here and apply the strategies to overcome them, you will continue to build a foundation for your company; whether you stay in Stage 3 or grow your business up to Stage 7, with 161 – 500 employees.

I know, because I've been there. As the owner and partner of a multi-million dollar company that I helped grow from two to over 100 employees, we struggled in Stage 3 for all of the reasons I cover in this book. In March of 2000, the false economy driven by the dot. com explosion collapsed. We had to lay off 30% of our staff and we struggled to stay afloat. Because we struggled, we lost critical traction.

When you lose traction, you create chaos. If I had known then what I know now, I firmly believe we would not have had to negatively impact 30 people's lives.

PREDICTING GROWTH

Through presenting the 7 Stages of Growth to CEOs around the country, I've encountered two consistent character traits.

1. People who start or run a company are smart, energetic, capable, able to think outside the box, willing to put in long hours, have a strong vision, believe 150% in their product or service, and feel overwhelmed most of the time.

2. They want a structure they can utilize to predict what is coming, how to manage the hundreds of issues that pop up every day and how to make sure they survive to the next stage of the business growth cycle.

During the journey through the 5 Challenges presented in Stage 3, I guarantee to help you:

1. Focus on the immediate issues in front of you.
2. Predict how growth will impact you.
3. Adapt to the changes your company is going through.

In the early stages of growing a company, you need to ask core questions such as:

1. How do I plan on targeting, capturing and caring for my customers?
2. Where do I find qualified people?
3. How do I keep exceptional people?
4. Am I tracking my revenue by revenue groups in order to understand where I generate the best margins?
5. Are we horizontally or vertically integrated?
6. What is our dominant culture?
7. What are our core processes?
8. Where do we see our company in three to five years?
9. How will we capture and encourage knowledge?
10. What is the relationship our company has with the customer, our vendors, our allies and our competitors?

This is book is designed to help a Stage 3 CEO understand where to focus his energies in order to get the most traction as he starts to build a successful company.

When James Fischer interviewed growth-smart companies in his 7 Stages of Growth research study, he was able to identify 27 specific challenges that business owners experienced as they grew. Business owners find value in these 27 challenges because they finally have a starting point to talk about what's going on in their business.

Fischer referred to these as the "stages of growth challenges." His premise was that CEOs should focus on these critical challenges at each stage of growth in order to minimize the chaos that can create obstacles to growth.

> *"What has occurred over the past 24 months has guided us to a new path for growth by building bench strength and a new leadership design for our company. Implementing the 7 Stages of Growth concepts has given us new insights to prepare us for organizational growth and internal development. The impacts on our organizational culture, the excitement of our store teams and our bottom line have all been affected positively."*
>
> -Richie Morgan, President Northern California Regional Grocery Chain – working with John Oakes, President of SBL Co., a certified Growth Curve Specialist

It's hard for business owners, bombarded by issues every day, to articulate what is going on for them. They know something is creating a problem, but they can't identify what it is. The 27 Challenges define in a few words what business owners are experiencing. That's a big step when you are trying to engage a team of people to help you fix something. The value of understanding the stages of growth is that throughout the model, we are guiding the CEO on how to prioritize their time, energy and dollars.

In Stage 3 companies, Fisher recognized that successful CEOs had figured out how to get and maintain staff buy-in. He realized that with 20 – 34 employees, the CEO had to start letting go to let the company grow beyond their own strengths. Those CEOs knew the importance of keeping those key employees aware of where the company was going and how their position—what they did every day—would help the company succeed. As your company grows, you will eventually have to tackle all 27 Challenges.

THE 27 CHALLENGES

1. Profits are inadequate to grow the company
2. Need for an improved profit design
3. Customers are migrating away from your products/ services
4. Continual cash flow challenges
5. Limited capital available to grow
6. Employee turnover
7. Hiring quality staff
8. Staff morale and voltage challenges
9. Need for a flexible planning model
10. Need to have better staff buy-in
11. Project management & resource coordination challenges
12. Leadership/staff communication gap
13. New staff orientation
14. Staff training
15. Unclear values throughout the organization
16. Dealing with the cost of lost expertise or knowledge when employees leave
17. Chaotic periods destabilize company

18. Organization needs to understand how the company will grow in the future, not just the leadership
19. Organization needs to better understand the impact that staff satisfaction has on the company's profitability
20. Company culture is generally resistant to change
21. The marketplace and your customers change too quickly
22. Difficulty forecasting problem areas before they surface
23. Difficulty diagnosing the real problems or obstacles to growth
24. Too slow getting new products/services to market
25. Not able to quickly get systems and procedures in place as the company is growing
26. Weak product/service development and differentiation in market
27. Challenge expanding sales

THE TOP 5 CHALLENGES OF A STAGE 3 COMPANY

The ability to help a CEO get clear about the right things at the right time is what separates high performing companies from mediocre companies. The small percentage of companies that succeed are the ones that tend to stay ahead of their growth curve.

The Top 5 Challenges for a Stage 3 Company, in this order, are:

1. Need to have better staff buy-in
2. Leadership/Staff communication gap
3. Need for an improved profit design
4. Unclear values throughout the organization
5. Company culture is generally resistant to change

Chapter 2:
Key Growth Concepts

As a company navigates through Stage 3, its primary goal is to determine if the business model you started with in Stage 1 and Stage 2 is still viable. A CEO should evaluate how the company will grow and think about the following foundational building blocks:

FUNCTION	BUILDING BLOCKS
Delegation System	Develop a system and template for delegation to insure you are building a team of confident, capable employees that can help you make decisions.
Quality Control	Implement a quality control review and feedback form to keep the team on track and held accountable.
Team/Staff	Your hiring system should identify the skills that are needed in specific positions and help you to find, recruit, select and hire great employees. You should also have a plan for each employee detailing expectations, performance measurements and actions that will help the company succeed.
Financial	Your financial system should include: (1) one-year profit plan (budget) projecting revenues and expenses; (2) financial model; (3) cash flow forecasting; and (4) dashboard.

Marketing/Sales	You should have a well-defined sales and marketing system that your sales people are using.
Support	Outsource part-time support such as COO, CFO and HR consultants.

There are three additional concepts central to the Stages of Growth language: the 4 Rules that govern the 7 Stages of Growth, understanding the Transition Zones between stages and the Three Gates of Focus. These concepts were discussed in Stages 1 and 2 as well.

THE FOUR RULES THAT GOVERN THE 7 STAGES OF GROWTH

As a business owner navigates their own growth curve, there are four rules that help to walk that fine line between chaos and equilibrium.

RULE #1:

THE MOVEMENT FROM ONE STAGE OF GROWTH TO ANOTHER BEGINS AS SOON AS YOU LAND IN ANY STAGE OF GROWTH.

You don't become a Stage 3 company overnight. As soon as you enter Stage 2, you begin to be a Stage 3 company. Think of the Stages of Growth as a continuum. You are moving along this continuum based on your strategic plan.

If you are a Stage 2 company today, and plan to have 25 employees on board in 18 months, NOW is the time to plan. This is what sets the 7 Stages of Growth apart from other business models. A CEO can actually *predict* when they will move into another stage of growth and adjust to upcoming needs *before* they arrive.

RULE #2:
WHAT YOU DON'T GET DONE IN A SPECIFIC STAGE OF GROWTH DOES NOT GO AWAY.

The challenges for your current stage of growth need to be addressed before you move into a new stage of growth. For example, if you established good cash flow procedures and tactics in Stage 2, you don't need to worry about them in Stage 3. A Top Stage 2 Challenge is hiring quality people. Did you put effective recruiting, interviewing and hiring processes in place, or are you still making critical missteps?

Business owners should consistently evaluate how well they are doing, not only with their current challenges, but also with the challenges that presented themselves in previous stages of growth. Too often, we resolve surface issues without uncovering the root cause.

Focus on your specific People, Process and Profit/Revenue challenges so that you are well prepared for tomorrow. Remember, the complexity of an organization will always extract its due. Don't be lulled into a false sense of security; there is always a price to pay for rapid growth.

RULE #3:
TIME WILL MAKE A DIFFERENCE.

Each stage of growth has its own set of challenges. If you are a Stage 3 company with 25 employees and you've been that way for 15 years, time has allowed you to grow slowly and address challenges as you grew. However, if you grew quickly, blew through Stages 1 and 2 and landed in Stage 3 overnight, there is a strong chance that the issues you should have addressed in Stage 2 remain unresolved.

The time rule applies to either slow or fast growth. It simply reminds you to pay attention to what you need to do as you grow through each stage of growth. A company that has been in one stage of growth for five years or more should look *ahead* to manage growth in a proactive way. Time makes a difference because slower growth is easier to manage.

Many companies choose to stay at a certain size. They prefer to grow in other dimensions, not in employees. Don't assume you have addressed your critical issues just because your business model limits the number of employees. Small companies are not immune to challenges simply because of low staff numbers.

RULE #4:
IF YOU AREN'T GROWING, YOU ARE DYING.

In order to stay fresh and current, something in your organization has to grow and change. The concept behind the stages of growth is similar to growth in nature, which has its own mechanisms to stir up the pot. A static condition in nature or in business is indicative of imminent death.

We are all familiar with the process a caterpillar goes through to turn into a butterfly. This is often described as one of the most intriguing transformations in the animal kingdom. If something goes wrong during the chrysalis stage, the butterfly will never emerge from the cocoon. Similarly, if the wheels start to come off a business in the early stages of growth, it may never recover.

As human beings, we have a tendency to gravitate toward a state of equilibrium because it is safe and understandable. In reality, if we stay in that state too long, it results in a slow dying away, just as it does in nature. Being able to get ahead of your growth curve allows you to recognize the signs of change and gives you time to react.

So, the answer to the question, "Do We Need to Grow?" is categorically YES. Even in a downturn economy when revenues are shrinking and profits melting away, there are areas of improvement a company can focus on.

The challenge for business owners in any stage of growth is to make sure they define growth for the company and not let growth define them.

CRITICAL TRANSITION ZONES

"Transition zones" exist between each stage of growth, which are actually phases of chaos an organization moves through in order to prepare itself for the next stage of growth. These transition zones are an important juncture in the growth model of any growth organization.

THE WIND TUNNEL

As your company moved from Stage 1 to Stage 2, it experienced a Flood Zone. The Flood Zone is a transition zone in which the level of activity increases to the point where people can feel like they are drowning. A company that is going through a Flood Zone has seen an increase in the number of employees, the amount of cash and revenue it has to manage, the number of clients, and the number of processes that need to be followed.

The Flood Zone forces you to find other ways of dealing with the workload. Examine your processes, examine your training programs, examine how you purchase materials, explore systems that track customer information and think about what positions you will need to hire when the time is right.

As a company moves from Stage 2 to Stage 3, it moves through a transition zone called a Wind Tunnel. It requires the leader to let go of methodologies that no longer work and acquire new ones that do.

In many ways, a Wind Tunnel can be even more challenging than a Flood Zone. I specifically remember when our company was in Stage 3 and our employees told us, in no uncertain terms, that we should "just lead"! My confusion was sincere. We had always been collaborative, ever since we started the company with just two employees. We prided ourselves on getting people's input when a decision had to be made. We still had a family type of atmosphere and we weren't hierarchical—everyone pitched in and got the job, whatever it was, done.

Our initial approach, leftover from Stage 1, was no longer working. In fact, our lack of roles and responsibilities, organization, and well-defined processes was driving our employees crazy. The altercation with the staff lasted for months as my business partner and I worked to restore their confidence in us as leaders. We tried to put our arms around a company that was growing faster than we could keep up with.

The message that finally sunk in for us was this: our employees wanted to be told what they needed to do to succeed. They weren't satisfied just doing what needed to be done. We were too big, and people were tripping all over each other. We had neglected to define critical jobs and roles. We thought people liked our approach because it allowed flexibility, but instead it created confusion and resentment.

In hindsight, I understand we went through a Wind Tunnel as we grew from Stage 2 (11 – 19 employees) to Stage 3 (20 – 34 employees). The methodologies that got us where we were no longer worked and we had to adapt new ones that worked for everyone. It was a hard concept to wrap our heads around.

We weathered our staff revolution and learned a lot of hard lessons from the experience. "Letting it go in order to grow" is a tough pill to swallow for most entrepreneurs, and we were no different.

Delegating responsibility and authority to key employees is critical during the third stage of growth. This is when many CEOs throw in the hat and decide to start over. They realize the managing of the business isn't what they love. Launching the idea is what drove them to succeed. They either have to become great managers or hire someone who loves managing the people side of the business.

Chaos is inevitable, but a good offense is better than a good defense. Take the time to explain to your staff what's going when the company transitions through a Wind Tunnel on its way to Stage 3. Don't assume they grasp the concept. Just because you understand the reality of growth and growing a business, doesn't mean your employees do. Be aware that your employees, who experience broken processes firsthand, need to feel empowered to identify issues that need to be fixed. You need to engage them in exploring how to improve the way work is done. Chances are, they're hesitant to bring up problems for fear of appearing incompetent, uninformed or critical.

A Wind Tunnel can create a language of growth, which allows employees to put a name to their pain and derive a measure of comfort. Utilize the language of growth to prepare employees for the chaos that comes with change.

THE THREE GATES OF FOCUS: PROFIT/REVENUE, PEOPLE AND PROCESS

CEOs can use the Three Gates of Focus (Profit/Revenue, People and Process) to clarify the root cause of issues. When a CEO identifies the root cause, and helps employees do the same, issues are resolved sooner. Every issue you face in your organization can be categorized under one of the Three Gates. They are always stacked in the order of importance for a particular stage of growth. In Stage 3, the top gate of focus is People.

The **People Gate** focuses on building competency, staff satisfaction, performance and innovation through the conscious development of people.

> Hiring and training
> Competitive benefits
> Ongoing, consistent training
> Employee engagement
> Vision, mission and core values
> Management training
> Leadership development
> Performance indicators
> Empowerment support

The **Profit/Revenue Gate** predicts growth by maximizing and anticipating profit/revenue and identifying capacity issues.

> Sales capacity
>
> Marketing capacity
>
> Facilities capacity
>
> Fulfillment capacity
>
> Capital availability
>
> Production capacity
>
> Product development capacity

The **Process Gate** helps transform complexity into clarity through processes.

> Sales processes
>
> Marketing processes
>
> Financial processes
>
> Customer service processes
>
> Operational processes
>
> Management processes
>
> Risk management processes

Let's look at an example. Lisa, a Stage 3 CEO, was told by one of her employees, Mike, that he was struggling with a project. Many CEOs blame the individual when there is a problem, instead of digging deeper to see if there is a process or a profit (can we afford it) issue.

To better understand Mike's struggle, Lisa asked, "Do you think the issue is People, Profit or Process related?"

This specific question forced Mike to think more seriously about the underlying issue and not just focus on what was showing up on the surface. Given the language, he may say that it's a People Issue and he needs more training; or he may identify that it's a Process Issue because the system they are using is no longer effective; or he may identify it as a Profit Issue, and explain that a critical piece of equipment is broken and needs to be replaced.

This brief but impactful conversation helped Lisa adopt a problem-solving approach and gave Mike a new way to approach the problem.

Language is the world's greatest change agent. Successful business owners instinctively know that you seed change in an enterprise by shifting and transforming the baseline language of the workplace community. People converse and communicate within the boundaries of the current language that describes their experience. Language doesn't just *describe* their experience; it *defines* it. Change the language and you change the experience.

For whatever reason, the financials of many businesses remains clouded in a language that confuses, rather than clarifies. Most people would prefer to leave this aspect up to the numbers people and be in the dark. Trying to explain a balance sheet to your employees is a little like trying to explain how an internal combustion engine works to someone who is not at all mechanically inclined. If, however, you explain there are drive mechanisms (spark plugs, gasoline, pistons, camshaft, transmission) that start the car moving forward, it all starts to make sense.

> Language doesn't just **describe** their experience; it **defines** it.

Adopt a similar approach when explaining to your employees that there are three ways to increase how much money you make: volume, price, and cost. You can increase the volume of what you sell, you can increase the sale price or decrease the production cost. Once your employees understand how they can directly impact these three factors, lights go on!

Suddenly, the financials are something they not only understand, but something they can talk about. The language shifts from the dry "earnings ratio to net profit" to a more engaged and educated interpretation. "We increased our price by 15%, increased our volume by 5%, decreased our costs by 20% and brought in an additional $50,000 in our first quarter." This is a powerful way to engage the entire company in understanding the financial impacts in your company.

One of the core values of the 7 Stages of Growth model is in its ability to help a company focus on the right things at the right time. The Gates of Focus allow everyone the opportunity to clarify issues quickly and reduce the chaos that comes with misdiagnosing a problem. In addition to providing clarity, the Three Gates of Focus begins the process of creating a language of growth. Throughout the 7 Stages, there are many opportunities for a CEO to help every employee understand what is going on in the company's growth cycle.

THREE GATES OF FOCUS FOR STAGE 1, STAGE 2 AND STAGE 3

STAGE 1 1-10 EMPLOYEES	STAGE 2 11 – 19 EMPLOYEES	STAGE 3 20 – 34 EMPLOYEES
Profit/Revenue Gate	Profit/Revenue Gate	People Gate
People Gate	Process Gate	Profit/Revenue
Process Gate	People Gate	Process

In Stage 3, the CEO must start delegating to capable people, become a more proficient manager and continue to clarify roles and responsibilities. With all those challenges ahead, it's no surprise that the top gate of focus for Stage 3 is People. While managing people is the most challenging aspect of growing a business, the reality is *people are your business*. Without capable, engaged and committed employees, the company will fail.

Chapter 3:
Hidden Agents

W hat is a Hidden Agent?

Hidden agents provide CEOs with a language to identify critical issues that may be creating obstacles to their growth. By understanding a company's hidden agents, a CEO can get to the root cause of a problem faster and engage their management team to focus on the right issues.

HIDDEN AGENT #1: BUILDER/ PROTECTOR RATIO

What do battlefield generals, sports coaches and successful business leaders all have in common? They all methodically measure key indicators that reveal the health of the human psyche inside their organizations. These indicators predict the organization's ability to win (or not win) on any given day.

Good leaders measure the ratio between their company's *confidence* and *caution* as it directly reflects the outcome of their performance efforts. Otherwise known as the Builder/Protector ratio, it provides insight into the true balance of confidence (Builder) and caution (Protector) inside a company. This measurement allows a CEO and their leadership team to assess the company's ability to accept change and successfully navigate the change.

If you own a business, you more than likely already understand a Builder mentality. You create new ideas, take on new initiatives and find ways to expand revenue and profitability. You choose to challenge and improve the way things are done, thrive on risk and support growth initiatives.

A Protector mindset is cautious and prefers to slow down the pace of change. They are risk averse and highly suspicious of growth. Protectors generally don't feel confident in the company's financial strength and are slow to embrace optimism for the future.

The optimal Builder/Protector Ratio during Stage 3 is 1:1. The ratio changes according to the stage of growth you're in, but no other stage is as balanced as 1:1.

BUILDERS:

- Create new ideas
- Take on new initiatives
- Find ways to expand revenue and profits
- Challenge the way things are done
- Are risk tolerant and highly supportive of growth
- Are highly confident
- Are always looking for new opportunities
- Don't back down from everyday challenges

PROTECTORS:

- Are cautious and slow paced
- Are risk averse
- May not feel confident in the company's financial strength
- Tend to be suspicious of new markets
- Prefer to apply the brakes (and should be encouraged to do so when appropriate)

Too much Protector, the company could stall. Too much Builder, the company could fail. Moving too slow or moving too fast makes managing more difficult and the top executive will struggle to gain buy-in.

The CEO must be a Builder and develop a like-minded team. However, the Protector mindset is helpful in small doses to counter the Builders' tendency toward over-inflated optimism.

> Too much Protector, the company could stall. Too much Builder, the company could fail.

DETERMINING YOUR COMPANY'S BUILDER/PROTECTOR RATIO

A leader can get a good idea of their company's Builder/Protector Ratio by:

1. Tuning into the voltage (think energy) in your company

2. Talking to the leadership team and asking pointed questions

3. Really listening to your employees

Get a read on your B/P Ratio by asking:

- Are people engaged in open and active dialogue?
- Are meetings productive and full of valuable information?
- Are good decisions being made?
- Does your leadership team and your employees appear optimistic about the future?
- Are they confident in the financial strength of the company?
- Do they have a high level of confidence in their co-workers?
- What are your employees saying?
- Is there behind-the-scenes gossiping?
- Is there a high rate of absenteeism or turnover?
- Do your managers or employees complain about a lack of accountability?
- Are projects often derailed or late?

If the company expands too fast and cash flow gets tight, you need to be the voice of caution. Pull back, rethink that next hire, or make a decision to expand the operation. Staying in the Protector mindset for too long isn't healthy for the organization, however.

You can move between the Builder/Protector mindset as the circumstances or situations require. Confidence need to be continually balanced with a certain amount of caution. The team will take its cues from you and how you respond to challenges.

• •

WHAT IS TOO MUCH?

While the results of a Builder mindset tend to manifest in ways that help a company grow (drive sales, look for new opportunities, strong financials), too much of a Builder mindset can create issues; just as a prolonged Protector mindset can restrict growth.

SYMPTOMS OF TOO MUCH BUILDER:

1) Hockey stick sales projections
2) Hiring in advance of need
3) Taking on high-risk projects without proper reward
4) Over-committing and under-delivering
5) Lack of clarity in the direction of the company

SYMPTOMS OF TOO MUCH PROTECTOR:

1) Unwilling to try new marketing and business development techniques
2) Too much focus on expenses, not enough on revenue
3) Sees hurdles instead of opportunities
4) Insulated, not seeking divergent opinions
5) Fearful about the future
6) Lack of communication

7) Hesitant to embrace change

8) Decisions take too long and opportunities are missed

• •

Understanding your company's Builder/Protector Ratio improves your insight into your company's mental health by:

1. Measuring the company's ability to meet and overcome challenges.
2. Communicating the company's willingness to perceive and take advantage of opportunities in its path.
3. Measuring the strength of the company's immune defense system, acting as a barrier against low morale and poor performance.
4. Assessing the company's willingness to advance itself through change.
5. Gauging the company's belief in its future.
6. Communicating the company's trust in its leaders.

WHEN THE BUILDER/PROTECTOR RATIO IS OUT OF ALIGNMENT

Too much confidence in Stage 3 and there is the risk of falling back on what worked in the past, which does nothing but throw the company into further chaos and disruption. CEOs tend to burn out when they try to control an enterprise that has outgrown their own individual capabilities.

Take a step back to examine and implement new methodologies or leadership styles. Loosen up on the Builder mentality to allow others within the organization to step up and take on more responsibility. You hired a team of experts. Now is the time to let them do their thing.

Too much caution (not letting go) in Stage 3 can cause employees to feel powerless at a time when they need to take charge. The outcome is low employee morale, low productivity, high turnover, loss of momentum, and a loss of confidence in leadership. While it's important to be cautious, too much caution can send a negative message.

I'll give you an example of how the Builder/Protector Ratio plays out in a Stage 3 enterprise. The Hammond Company, a service-based business, found itself struggling to maintain momentum when it left Stage 2.

ISSUES INCLUDED:

1. A CEO used to maintaining control, suddenly overwhelmed by trying to maintain a level of sales to support a growing enterprise.
2. A widening gap between what the CEO wanted and how the employees behaved.
3. Employees struggled to take on more responsibility without the necessary authority.
4. A CEO uneasy about giving up decision-making control, which caused employees to question their roles.
5. Employees unsure about their every move who wondered why the CEO didn't trust them.

6. A lack of focus on company values, which allowed bad behaviors to go unchecked and caused friction among the staff.
7. Profits eroded due to inattention to rising overhead costs without swift price adjustments.
8. Lack of a strong strategic growth plan, which caused employees to question the CEO's ability to manage the chaos.

The Hammond Company was on the edge of a staff rebellion and the CEO was on the verge of burnout. Will it happen right away? No. Many companies continue to expand and grow with the issues outlined above.

Giving up control of different aspects within a company is extremely challenging. The CEO knew he had to hire quality people and drive strong sales to support higher wages. His frustration was fueled when his capable employees seemed to shrink from responsibility instead of embrace it.

What did this CEO do wrong? He overlooked the management piece. He had no problem handing out assignments, but he neglected to set and manage expectations. When the team didn't deliver as he had hoped, his disappointment showed, which caused the team to retract into a caution/Protector mentality. He thought they were unmotivated and unwilling to step up. He should have taken the time to educate them about plans for the future, the current financial health of the organization and how they fit onto the company's long-term success plan.

The Hammond Company is a classic example of what happens when the Builder/Protector Ratio is out of whack. When the Ratio is out of alignment, the CEO can send a signal to the team that he is not confident about the direction of the company, without even being aware of it. That lack of confidence manifests in key employees or the management team, and ultimately ricochets throughout the entire company.

Finding the right balance between a Builder and Protector mindset is key to surviving Stage 3. The CEO needs to provide strong direction, set expectations and manage to those expectations. The goal is to guide, manage, direct, coach, encourage and correct, which is how a CEO demonstrates a balance between confidence and caution.

Employees want direction. They also want to be valued and feel that what they do every day has meaning. Once a CEO and his team understands the Builder/Protector Ratio, the dynamic in a growing company can change within weeks.

THE BUILDER/PROTECTOR RATIO FOR STAGE 1, STAGE 2 AND STAGE 3

STAGE 1 (1 – 10 EMPLOYEES)	STAGE 2 (11 – 19 EMPLOYEES)	STAGE 3 (20 – 34 EMPLOYEES
4:1	3:1	1:1

HIDDEN AGENT #2: THREE FACES OF A LEADER

The 7 Stages of Growth research uncovered the Three Faces of a Leader. The length of time a leader spends wearing one of these faces depends upon their stage of growth. There is a model percentage blend for each stage.

For a Stage 3 company, the Three Faces blend looks like this:

VISIONARY: 10%

Visionary leaders ensure the company knows where it wants to go. They can take the most insignificant situation and turn it into an opportunity. It's important that leaders in Stage 3 continue to share the vision and continually check in with their growing number of employees to help keep that vision alive. As with Stage 2, there is still a lot of chaos and uncertainty within a Stage 3 company. In the chaos of growth, employees can lose sight of the bigger picture and question why they are doing what they are doing.

Spend time talking with each employee about how they see the company and find out what they think the company's strengths and weaknesses are. Help them to see themselves in the future of the organization, and challenge them to continually grow and learn in order to help the company do the same.

MANAGER: 60%

The manager face understands the importance of growing a company through the management of workflow and people. A manager creates order and focuses on pragmatic systems and procedures that make the company run well. This requires emotional intelligence and dedication to helping people succeed.

The manager face has increased from 20% in Stage 2 to 60% in Stage 3—it's a critical lynchpin in running a successful Stage 3 company. "Letting it go to let it grow" is all about surrounding yourself with people who are better at certain tasks and functions than you are.

When you hire skilled, experienced people, they need to be able to utilize those skills and experience. Getting through Stage 3 successfully hinges on learning to manage people well.

SPECIALIST: 30%

The specialist face represents the work the company produces. Specialists understand the need to capture the necessary processes, to deliver the work and meet clients' needs. In most cases, the specialist is the person who came up with the idea to start the company; he is action oriented and detail focused.

If the CEO has taken a strong role in developing the product or service, now is the time to help employees gain ownership of the role they play in delivering that product or service to customers.

Because the leader understands their product or service better than anyone else, it's easy to default to hands-on development or working directly with customers. Your employees need to take a more active role, however, you don't have to have all the answers anymore!

THREE FACES OF A LEADER FOR STAGE 1, STAGE 2 AND STAGE 3

STAGE 1 (1 – 10 EMPLOYEES)	
VISIONARY	40%
MANAGER	10%
SPECIALIST	50%

STAGE 2 (11 – 19 EMPLOYEES)	
VISIONARY	40%
MANAGER	20%
SPECIALIST	40%

STAGE 3 (20 – 34 EMPLOYEES)	
VISIONARY	10%
MANAGER	60%
SPECIALIST	30%

THE THREE FACES AT WORK

A CEO of a growing company needs to bring all three faces (Visionary, Manager and Specialist) to the table every day. The three faces provide the much needed focus to clarify roles and responsibilities for each and every position. Identify capable employees who can take on more responsibility and help those employees become confident in their abilities.

You'll also need to focus on the financial side of your business. Make sure you have a profit plan in place, are monitoring cash flow weekly and have established key indicators for all aspects of the company. The ability to handle critical conversations and not let poor performance go unnoticed is important. Follow up and verify that what needs to be done is being done to your satisfaction.

A CEO who believes that employees come to the table to succeed and embraces his role as manager in Stage 3 will successfully navigate their growth curve. Take the time to focus on the needs of your people. Ask people for their insight and ideas before providing answers. Find out what their goals and dreams are. Remember, your people ARE your business. Understanding how to manage them is essential.

HIDDEN AGENT #3: LEADERSHIP STYLE

Leaders create resonance in an organization by ensuring the entire fabric of a company is laced with emotional intelligence. Developing a new leadership style means changing how one operates with other people.

What do winning leaders have in common?

- They are aware of their own emotions and attuned with empathy toward the people they lead.
- They understand that handling relationships well begins with authenticity.

If a leader acts disingenuously or manipulatively, for instance, their team will immediately sense a note of falseness, which leads to distrust. The ability to connect emotionally to the people you lead is important for an environment that fosters involvement and commitment from everyone in your company.

KEY LEADERSHIP STYLES

The six Leadership Styles from Daniel Goleman's incredibly useful book, *Primal Leadership: Unleashing the Power of Emotional Intelligence* are summarized here for your reference.

1. **Visionary:** Visionary leaders frame the collective task in terms of a grander vision. Employees are encouraged to innovate and work toward shared goals that build team commitment. People are proud to belong to the organization.

2. **Coaching:** Coaching leaders communicate a belief in people's potential and an expectation they will do their best. By linking people's daily work to long-term goals, coaches keep people motivated.

3. **Affiliative:** Affiliative leaders recognize employees as people and put less emphasis on accomplishing tasks and goals. Such leaders build tremendous loyalty and strengthen connectedness.

4. **Democratic:** A democratic leader builds on a triad of primal leadership abilities: teamwork and collaboration, conflict management and influence. Listening is the key strength of this "team member" leadership style.

5. **Pacesetting:** A pacesetter leader holds and exemplifies high standards for performance. The primal leadership foundation of this style lies in

the drive to achieve by continually finding ways to improve their own performance and that of those they lead.

6. **Commanding:** Commanding leaders draw on three primal leadership competencies: influence, achievement and initiative. They exert forceful direction to get better results and opportunities are seized in an unhesitating tone.

Great leaders move us. They ignite our passion and inspire the best in us. When people try to explain great leadership they talk about vision, strategy and powerful ideas. The reality is great leadership works through emotions. It's *how* you connect to people that leads to success.

Your job as a leader just got harder or easier, depending on how you want to look at it. You have the power to sway everyone's emotions. If you push people with enthusiasm and open communication, performance will soar. If you drive them with rancor and anxiety, they will return in kind.

The reason a leader's manner – not just *what* he does but *how* he does it – matters so much lies in the design of the human brain: what scientist have started to call the "open loop" of our emotional centers. A closed loop system, such as the circulatory system, is self-regulating. What's happening in the circulatory system of those around us does not impact our own system.

> **If you push people with enthusiasm and open communication, performance will soar.**

An open loop system depends largely on external sources to manage itself.

In other words, we rely on connections with other people for our own emotional stability. In intensive care units, research has shown that the comforting presence of another person not only lowers the patient's blood pressure, but also slows the secretion of fatty acids that block arteries.

Here's a startling statistic: three or more incidents of intense stress within a year (financial trouble, being fired or a divorce) triple the death rate in socially isolated, middle aged men. Alternatively, incidents of stress have zero impact on the death rate of men who cultivate close relationships.

This open loop system says "people need people." The ability of a leader to connect to their people at work can have the same healthy results as when that emotional awareness is taken home.

STYLES NEED TO BE PRACTICED AND ADJUSTED

Leadership is a skill like any other. Anyone who has the will and the motivation can become a better leader. Understanding the steps and taking the time to practice can turn a mediocre leader into one who inspires greatness. Improvement starts with understanding where you are today and what you aspire to be. That's why a solid diagnosis of your leadership strengths and weaknesses and a plan for development are crucial. Tuned-out, dissonant leaders are one of the main reasons that talented people leave a company, taking precious knowledge with them.

Our guiding values are represented in the pre-frontal areas of the brain as a hierarchy; what we love is at the top and what we loathe is at the bottom. What keeps us moving toward our goals comes down to the mind's ability to remind us how satisfied we will feel when we accomplish them.

What does this mean to you as a leader? Wherever people gravitate within their work role indicates where their real pleasure lies. That pleasure is itself motivating. External motivations don't get people to perform at their absolute best–it's an inside job!

Why should you care? By tuning into the desires, dreams and career goals of your employees, you gain insight into what motivates them. If you can take their passion and turn it into a driving force in their jobs, you've started to build a company that can truly go from being good to great.

To succeed, leadership development must be the strategic priority of the enterprise. Understanding the six leadership styles and how they impact each stage of growth is a powerful tool for any CEO. In the 7 Stages of Growth model, there are three critical leadership styles for each stage of growth. They are stacked in order of importance.

The top leadership styles for a Stage 3 leader are Coaching, Democratic and Pace-setting. A successful leader must be able to bring all three styles into play based on the situation, but in Stage 3, Coaching is the most effective style.

> Leadership development must be the strategic priority of the enterprise.

WHAT DOES A COACHING STYLE LOOK LIKE?

When you utilize a Coaching style, your role is to connect an individual's goals with the company's goals. Coaching leaders motivate and enhance employee performance by building long-term capabilities and self-confidence. While Coaching is the most effective style, it is also the least used. Patience and a willingness to learn the art of delegation are required and too often, leaders feel the need to solve instead of teach or listen.

This story from *Primal Leadership*, by Daniel Goleman, illustrates how effective a Coaching style can be.

> She was new at the firm and eight months pregnant. Staying late one night, she looked up from her work and was startled to see her boss standing at her door. He asked how she was doing, sat down, and started talking with her. He wanted to know all about her life. How did she like her job? Where did she want to go in her career? Would she come back to work after she had the baby?

> These conversations continued daily over the next month until the woman had her baby. The boss was David Ogilvy, the legendary advertising executive. The pregnant newcomer was Shelley Lazarus, now CEO of Ogilvy & Mather, the huge ad agency that Ogilvy founded. One of the main reasons Lazarus says she's still here, decades later, is the bond she forged with mentor Ogilvy in those first after-hour conversations.

Today, Shelley Lazarus is Chairman Emeritus of Ogilvy & Mather. Her love for the company she helped to build and for the man who taught her what running a business is all about is strong to this day.

> Of all the things we talked about, I remember most what he said about people. He said to me: "You can never spend too much time thinking about, worrying about and caring about your people because, at the end of the day, it's only the people who matter. Nothing else. If you always hire people who are smaller than you are, we shall become a company of dwarfs. If, on the other hand, you always hire people who are bigger than you are, we shall become a company of giants.

Coaching leaders not only retain talented people, they build an organization that encourages accountability and transparency. A leader who uses the Coaching style helps employees uncover answers and solutions, identify their unique strengths and weaknesses, and ties those attributes to their personal and career aspirations. They help employees conceptualize a plan for reaching goals, while being specific about their own responsibility as well as the employees. Coaching isn't hand holding, it's giving someone a hand.

Larry Bossidy, co-author of *Execution: The Art of Getting Things Done*, believes good coaching is about trying to impart experience. In his article "The Art of Good Coaching," he says, "You try to point out the best way of doing something, not because you are so smart, but because you've seen it 100 times." Bossidy believes that if he helps people find a better way of doing something, he's contributing to their overall

> **Coaching isn't hand holding, it's giving someone a hand.**

success, which is what coaching is all about. Conversely, if your people don't get better, it's your fault too. The article goes on to say, "Coaching and performance are intricately tied." You can get short-term performance by dictating what needs to be done or you can create an environment where people are continually coached to deliver great performance.

Coaching is a two-way street. You need to listen to how people respond. A good coach has great interpersonal skills, is a good communicator and knows when to press and when to praise. They show people how their participation fits into the overall goals of the company.

A Coaching leader is good at delegating and gives employees goals that stretch them, not just tasks that get a job done. Coaching works best with employees who show initiative and are looking for opportunities to improve. A surprisingly positive emotional impact stems from the leader's willingness to communicate a belief in people's potential. Leaders who have a high degree of empathy, who listen first before reacting or giving feedback, often ask themselves, "Is this about my issue or goal, or theirs?"

In Simon Synek's book, *Start With Why*, he talks about how most companies understand *what* they do. They make sure they have a value proposition that describes *how* they do it, but the challenge for many organizations is helping people understand the *why*. In Synek's research great leaders work from the inside out. They start with the *why* and make sure every single person in the company understands that *why* too. The Coaching style supports this "inside out" approach, which is why this style is the most effective tool a leader can bring to their organization.

WHAT DOES A DEMOCRATIC STYLE LOOK LIKE?

A Democratic leadership style builds resonance in an organization by valuing employee's input and getting commitment through participation. The greatest risk for any leader is to be out of touch with what is going on. Honing your skills as a Democratic leader builds on a triad of emotional intelligence abilities: teamwork and collaboration, conflict management and influence.

Democratic leaders focus on building trust and respect by getting staff buy-in. This style is particularly useful when the leader is uncertain about what direction to take and needs to solicit ideas from able employees. Because of its collaborative nature, this style is effective for keeping morale high. Democratic leaders know how to quell conflict and create a sense of harmony.

> Democratic leaders focus on building trust and respect by getting staff buy-in.

The best communicators are superb listeners, and listening is the key strength of Democratic leaders. They truly want to hear employee's thoughts and ideas. They work as a team member, rather than top down leaders. When faced with difficult situations, they bring people together, identify the problem and listen to what people say. This may take several iterations of working with different groups, but they allow key people to help determine solutions.

A Democratic leadership style promotes a willingness to hear all aspects of a problem, good and bad, without judging or shutting people down. This style encourages a safe environment, where all ideas and suggestions are heard and discussed.

The Democratic style has a few downsides, however. There can be a tendency to rely too heavily on endless meetings to find consensus. Sometimes, decisions are put off as a result, which can cause confusion. A lack of direction can erode employee enthusiasm. There are times when quick decisions are required, but good leaders know when to act swiftly and when to enlist the team.

WHAT DOES A PACESETTING STYLE LOOK LIKE?

The Pacesetting style focuses on high performance. It can look like micromanaging, because there is an emphasis on immediate, short-term goals, such as sales numbers.

Used sparingly, this style can help set the standard for excellence, especially if the leader exemplifies that excellence in their actions, not just their words. According to Goleman, "Pacesetting makes sense in particular during the entrepreneurial phase of a company's life cycle, when growth is all important." When a team is highly competent, motivated and needs little direction, this style can be effective.

The challenge for a Pacesetting leader is to know when to back off. Pacesetters tend to be unclear about setting expectations and establishing guidelines. They are results-focused and can come off as uncaring, which causes employees to feel they are being pushed too hard or worse, that the leader doesn't trust them. The more pressure they put on people for results, the more anxiety it provokes. Morale can plummet under a strict Pacesetting leader and poor performance will become the norm. When people lose sight of the vision, the exceptional employees will leave.

This style needs to be balanced with the Coaching style, so people remain motivated. To achieve sustainable growth, expectations must be defined and managed. Pacesetting leaders must continually find ways to improve performance, which means seizing opportunities. When leaders show initiative combined with goal setting, Pacesetting becomes a strength and not a weakness.

LEADERSHIP STYLES FOR STAGE 1, STAGE 2 AND STAGE 3

STAGE 1 (1-10 EMPLOYEES)	STAGE 2 (11 – 19 EMPLOYEES)	STAGE 3 (20 – 24 EMPLOYEES)
VISIONARY	COACHING	COACHING
COACHING	PACESETTING	DEMOCRATIC
COMMANDING	COMMANDING	PACESETTING

WHEN LEADERSHIP STYLE IS OUT OF ALIGNMENT

The ability to effectively utilize all six leadership styles is what distinguishes an emotionally aware leader from a leader who elects to focus more on tasks than people. Business owners feel a tremendous sense of urgency when launching a new product or service. The pressure forces the leader to be more direct and there can be a tendency to micro-manage in the early stages of growth. A Pacesetting or Commanding style may work in the short term but not in the long term.

When a company moves into Stage 3 and needs to focus on how to encourage people to take on new and different roles and responsibilities, the ability to listen and teach, not direct, is critical. A leader who is unable or unwilling to release control will send a negative message to capable employees, causing those employees to question their value and their roles. Just when that leader needs to rely on others, his own inability to adjust his leadership style to the needs of the company, can derail growth and undermine trust. When leaders hide behind their own failings, good companies become poisonous environments and very rarely recover.

Developing a new leadership style means learning to change how you operate with people. The first step in this journey is to honestly assess your effectiveness today. Leadership development isn't a program; it's a strategic initiative that needs to permeate a culture and encourage personal development, starting at the top. By understanding all six of the leadership styles and adjusting their leadership style to each stage of growth, a CEO will be better prepared for the changes that come as the company adds employees.

> Leadership development isn't a program; it's a strategic initiative.

Take the Leadership Style Assessment to identify your strengths and weaknesses.

LEADERSHIP STYLE ASSESSMENT

Directions: Within each grouping of six statements please select the statement that most represents your leadership style and put the #6 after it. Then select your second choice by assigning it a #5. Then select your third choice by assigning it a #4 and so on until you select your last choice by assigning it a # 1.

A. Your leadership style helps the organization understand where it is going. _____

B. Your leadership style helps people identify their unique strengths and weaknesses and tying those to personal and career aspirations. _____

C. Your leadership style helps people repair broken trust in the organization._____

D. Your leadership style is based on genuinely listening to people. _____

E. Your leadership style is based on a high standard of excellence. _____

F. Your leadership style is based on a decisive commanding presence that people can trust. _____

A. People feel pride in the organization as a result of your values and vision. _____

B. People believe that your advice is genuinely in their best interest. _____

C. People experience greater harmony, better communication and improved morale based on your leadership abilities. _____

D. People believe that you can settle any conflict. _____

E. People feel a drive to improve their performance in your company. _____

F. People under your leadership have clear guidelines and understand what is expected of them. _____

A. As a result of your leadership style people see how their work fits into the big picture. _____

B. As a result of your leadership style people have a sense that you believe in them and that you expect their very best effort. _____

C. As a result of your leadership style people feel they are more important to you than the task they are doing. _____

D. As a result of your leadership style people believe they are really a part of an overall team. _____

E. As a result of your leadership style people feel a need to create new opportunities for the company. _____

F. As a result of your leadership style people feel confident that someone is in charge. _____

YOUR TOP LEADERSHIP STYLE

Thanks for taking the Leadership Styles Assessment. Once you have captured your scores and placed them in the appropriate area below, look at the 'key' section to determine what your top leadership style is based on where you are today. Remember, leadership styles are situational. The value in identifying your leadership style and comparing it with where you are in your stage of growth is to help you understand if your leadership style is a hidden agent that may be hindering your ability to help your company grow.

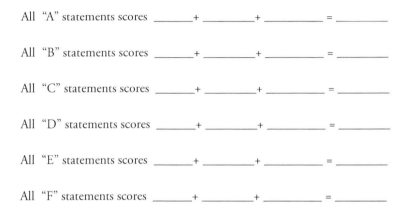

All "A" statements scores _____ + _____ + _____ = _____

All "B" statements scores _____ + _____ + _____ = _____

All "C" statements scores _____ + _____ + _____ = _____

All "D" statements scores _____ + _____ + _____ = _____

All "E" statements scores _____ + _____ + _____ = _____

All "F" statements scores _____ + _____ + _____ = _____

THE KEY TO YOUR LEADERSHIP STYLES:

A score = Visionary: The Visionary Leader is particularly effective when changes, even a business turnaround, require a new vision or clarifying a new direction. People are motivated by Visionary Leadership toward shared dreams that resonate with a company's values, goals and mission.

B score = Coaching: The Coaching Leader connects what a person wants with the company's goals. A good Coaching Leader motivates and enhances employee performance by building long term capabilities and self-confidence. It is by getting to know their employees on a deeper, personal level that these leaders make that link a reality.

C score = Affiliative: An Affiliative Leader creates harmony by connecting people to each other, often healing rifts in a team, providing motivation during stressful times or strengthening connections. The focus is on the emotional needs of employees over works goals. This empathy allows a leader to care for the whole person and boosts morale par excellence.

D score = Democratic: A Democratic Leader values people's input and they get commitments through participation. They typically are attuned to a wide range of people and they build consensus when unclear about which direction to take. This often generates fresh ideas for executing it.

E score = Pacesetting: Pacesetting Leaders meet challenging and exciting goals to get high-quality results from a motivated and competent team. These leaders require initiative and the hyper-vigilant readiness to create opportunities to do better and meet goals. This leadership style's continual high pressure performance zone can be debilitating for employees. These leaders typically lack self-awareness or the ability to collaborate or communicate effectively hence employee morale plummets and a total lack of trust ensues.

F score = Commanding: In a crisis, this leadership style can kick-start a turn-around and allay fears by providing crystal clear direction. A Commanding Leader is highly successful at unfreezing useless business habits or ruts and they relentlessly drive for better results. A legacy of the old command-and-control hierarchies that typified 20th century businesses, this military approach is truly appropriate to the battlefield, hospital emergency room or a hostile takeover.

Largest number is your dominant style. Second largest number is your secondary style. Third largest number is your auxiliary style. In case of a tie, you need to declare a preference between the styles. Based on the work of Daniel Goleman, Richard Boyatzis and Annie McKee, Primal Leadership, Harvard Universit.

HIDDEN AGENT #4: NON-NEGOTIABLE LEADERSHIP RULES

Getting focused on the right things at the right time spells success for any leader of a growing organization. Getting an entire team of people focused on the right things at the right time is what takes good companies and makes them great.

The 7 Stages of Growth research has provided us with rules of the road that help business owners focus on critical aspects of their company as they move through the different stages of growth. Each stage of growth offers 5 Non-Negotiable Leadership Rules that give business owner's specific guidelines on what they need to take seriously in terms of activities designed to create a solid foundation on which to grow. As the President of a company that grew beyond my expectations, I struggled to find ways to engage employees in understanding what was needed to manage that growth. However, once I began to understand the stages of growth and could articulate the rules of the road, that challenge became easier to manage. Why? Because I was talking a language each employee in my company could understand.

Growing a business demands every minute of your energy, resources and brain power. The good news is you don't have to reinvent the wheel. By understanding your stage of growth, by knowing what the rules of the road are for each stage of growth, you will have headlights to help you navigate the curves and get ahead of the obstacles. One thing we have learned. What you don't get done in your current stage of growth will simply not just go away. The rules in each stage of growth need to be addressed and if they aren't, you will face them again as you move to the next stage of growth.

As you read through the rules of the road for a Stage 1 - 3 company, you'll have tools you can use to help your entire company begin to understand what is needed from everyone to succeed.

STAGE 1 LEADERSHIP RULES OF THE ROAD – 1 – 10 EMPLOYEES:

RULE #1:
GENERATE, TRACK AND PRESERVE CASH.

Do you receive a daily report that tells you how you are doing on your company key indicators?

Do you have a simple budget and a 6 – 8 week rolling cash flow system to help you manage your company's cash?

Are you focused on getting new customers and increasing the transaction value and the frequency of those transactions to build your top line revenue?

RULE #2:
FOCUS 80% OF YOUR RESOURCES ON SELLING THE 2 – 3 OFFERINGS WITH THE BEST MARGINS.

Are you focusing 80% of your marketing, sales and customer service resources on your 3 top offerings?

Are you tracking your production output?

Do you know what your cost of goods and gross margins are on your products and service offerings sold?

RULE #3:
HIRE FIRST FOR 'HOW THE PERSON FITS IN WITH THE TEAM' AND SECOND FOR HOW COMPETENT THEY ARE.

Do you have a clear profile of the criteria that makes a good company fit?

Do you have clearly defined roles and responsibilities for all staff positions?

Do you have a standard interview process that you use to screen new job applicants?

RULE #4:
EMBRACE CHAOS – COMMAND THE TEAM AND INSPIRE THE EMPLOYEES.

Do you consistently set the company's priorities and clearly communicate them to your staff?

Have you clearly articulated the company's vision for the future and regularly communicate it to your staff?

Have you insured that your team has a clear mission, a clear set of instructions and practical goals to reach?

RULE #5:
ESTABLISH A PERFORMANCE MINDSET, A COMMUNICATION FEEDBACK LOOP AND EMPLOYEE DEVELOPMENT PROGRAM.

Have you established clear performance expectations with every employee?

Do you have an employee skill development program in place?

Do you consistently gather and give feedback to your employees?

STAGE 2 LEADERSHIP RULES OF THE ROAD – 11 - 19 EMPLOYEES:

RULE #1:
SELL ABSOLUTELY EVERY DAY.

Do you organize your schedule to sell every day?

Have you set up an effective sales process?

Do you have a contact management system in place to effectively follow up with leads, prospects and clients?

RULE #2:
DEVELOP, WITHOUT FAIL, THREE EMPLOYEE LEADERS TO BE RESPONSIBLE, ACCOUNTABLE AND PROACTIVE.

Have you defined clear roles of responsibility with three supervisor candidates?

Do you meet weekly one-on-one with these supervisors to support their commitment to performance-based goals?

Do you reward these key supervisors when they proactively demonstrate signs of leadership?

RULE #3:
CREATE A DAILY, WEEKLY AND MONTHLY KEY INDICATOR INSTRUMENT PANEL/FLASH SHEET.

Have you determined key health indicators for each department in your company?

Have you organized a system to engage the daily collection of key health indicator data from staff?

Have you formulated a daily, weekly and monthly flash sheet system report you can review regularly?

RULE #4:
COMMUNICATE ANY AND ALL DIRECTIONS IN WRITING.

Have you set up a simple CEO memo system template when communicating with staff that sets priority level of tasks, purpose, objectives and directions?

Do you have a retrieval system for all written memo directions?

Do you use the written memos during work performance reviews?

RULE #5:
DRIVE SMALL ACTION TEAMS TO HIT GOALS.

Do you set clear and agreed upon action team goals?

Do you organize and facilitate crisp action team meetings?

Do you organize/review regular team action lists and delegate tasks and due dates?

STAGE 3 LEADERSHIP RULES OF THE ROAD – 20 - 34 EMPLOYEES:

RULE #1:
DELEGATE RESPONSIBILITY AND AUTHORITY TO CAPABLE SUPERVISORS AND MEET WITH THEM REGULARLY.

Have you appointed a supervisory team and do you meet with them weekly?

At these meetings, do you delegate, track and review specific authority and responsibility to each supervisor?

Have you identified and developed a company-wide daily key indicator system?

RULE #2:
CREATE A FINANCIAL REPORTING AND PROJECTION SYSTEM.

Have you organized your profit and loss statement based on revenue groups?

Have you developed a weekly cash flow report?

Do you have a profit plan and are you reviewing it monthly with key employees?

RULE #3:
INSTILL A TEAM-BASED MINDSET THROUGHOUT THE COMPANY.

Have you created a team credo?

Have you outlined clear roles and responsibilities for all team members?

Have you identified the values that will drive behavior and instill accountability?

RULE #4: OVERHAUL THE BUSINESS MODEL.

Recently, have you challenged all assumptions regarding vision, mission, goals, objectives and strategies of the company?

Do you regularly challenge all assumptions about the customer, the competition, the market and your company's offerings?

Are you focused on reorganizing the company's resources to meet the new business design conclusions?

RULE #5: WITHOUT FAIL, CLARIFY AND STRENGTHEN ANY AND ALL COMMUNICATION WITH YOUR EMPLOYEES.

Do you clearly communicate the goals and direction of the company to all employees?

Have you established and demonstrated the company's core guiding values, preferably with input from your employees?

Are you consistently meeting one-on-one with direct reports each week?

These rules of the road will fundamentally drive your business to succeed. By keying in on these critical elements for your current stage of growth, you'll begin to proactively manage your growth, instead of letting growth manage you.

Spend time answering each question under each rule – don't gloss over them thinking they don't affect you. You don't have to reinvent how to manage growth. By spending time every day on these rules of the road you'll watch productivity increase and profits grow.

Chapter 4:
Delegation Unplugged

"People and organizations don't grow much without delegation and completed staff work because they are confined to the capacities of the boss and reflect both personal strengths and weaknesses."
– Stephen Covey

The definition from Webster's dictionary states, "When you delegate, you empower someone else to act for you. The act of delegation, then, involves conferring (some of) your functions or powers on another so he or she can act on your behalf."

We all GET what delegation is all about. No one refutes the necessity of it. Why, then is it so darn hard to do? In my own personal experience, delegation became easier as I became a better leader. In order to build an organization, you have to learn how to manage people and tasks. That, in my opinion, is what delegation is all about. If you can't delegate, you aren't managing. If you aren't managing, you aren't leading.

Nothing creates more problems for an entrepreneur than "conferring your functions or powers" on someone else. If it were easy, small business would not have an 80% attrition rate. If you fail at learning how to delegate effectively, you lose. Period.

Delegation involves knowing what should be delegated; it requires a clear set of expectations and a follow-up process.

Do any of these sentiments sound familiar?

- "Every time I delegate something, it backfires and I end up doing it over again!"
- "Delegate? What if they mess up?"
- "Why is it so hard to expect people to get something done the way you want it done?"
- "I hate to delegate! I'm always disappointed with the results!"
- "Who has time to delegate? By the time I explain what I want done, I could have it done already!"
- "Delegation only works with people who are really motivated to succeed."
- "Delegating is a great concept, but I'm tired of trying to teach my employees how to get the work done."
- "Why can't my managers step-up and take the initiative? I have to do everything!"

I've heard them all. Having helped grow a startup to over 120 employees, I understand the challenge of delegation. However, no business became successful without the leader learning how to delegate.

Ron Price, co-author of *The Complete Leader*, and president and CEO of Price & Associates, believes that since no one can give us more time, the only way we as leaders can maximize what we have, is by becoming effective at delegation:

> *"There is a big difference between delegating and dumping. Dumping your tasks on someone says, 'I'm stressed; I don't want to take care of this. I'm just going to hand it to you and forget about it.' This isn't a very collaborative way to get work done, and it doesn't invite engagement, trust or high-quality work. By contrast, delegation says, 'I believe that by us working together as a team, you can do a better job of spearheading this task than I can, so I'm asking you to be a part of my team for this particular project. I believe that we can get a better result together.'"*

Every client I've worked with has struggled with this basic concept.

A SIMPLE FOUR-STEP APPROACH TO DELEGATION

STEP 1: ARTICULATE YOUR VISION

"He who has a why can endure any how."
– Friedrich Nietzsche

People need to understand the bigger picture and, more importantly, how what they do every day impacts the future of the organization. Why did you start your business? Where do you see your business in the next 18 – 24 months? What do you care about? What do you stand for? Why are you different/better than your competition? Without this clarity on your part, it's hard for your employees to understand why they should care.

IMPLEMENTATION IDEA:

Communicate the vision. Write it down. Talk about that vision every chance you get. In your weekly one-on-one with your direct reports, ask if they have any questions about where the organization is going. If they don't have an answer, supply one for them. Explain the vision again. And again. Then ask them how their job, what they do every day impacts how the organization is going to implement on that vision.

STEP 2: MAP THE ROUTE

Once you know where you want to go, then you need to decide what route to take. What positions, roles, responsibilities, talent and skills are needed to grow the company? You can't delegate if you don't know where you are going or how you will get there. Don't assume employees understand their roles and responsibility just because you pay them a lot of money or they have experience. They aren't mind readers. Your employees need to be told what their job is, what your expectations are, how doing their job impacts the organization, and what the consequences are if they don't do their job. Basic management. Sound leadership.

IMPLEMENTATION IDEA:

Create an organizational chart to identify what positions are needed to grow your business, how each position helps you attain your vision and identify specific roles and responsibilities. This isn't a people chart. If you already have people in certain roles, take them out of the equation. It's tempting to want certain people to stay in certain roles. Maybe they started with the organization and you feel obligated to have them around. That kind of thinking clouds your judgment.

STEP 3: FOLLOW UP

Following up helps people accept accountability. And trying to delegate tasks without follow up is like trying to lose weight without changing any behaviors. It won't work.

If employees understand their roles and are responsible for specific tasks, the delegation conversation becomes much easier. "We agreed you would have the sales procedures in place no later than May 30. Thanks for getting back to me with your results." Delegating requires follow up to ensure assignments are completed. "I see you didn't get the sales process completed by the 30th. What was the reason and what's your new plan to get us back on track?" Bad managers micromanage. Exceptional managers delegate effectively. Which one are you?

IMPLEMENTATION IDEA:

Improve your management and leadership skills. An organization will only rise to the level of the leaders' ability. John Maxwell, author of *21 Irrefutable Laws of Leadership*, calls this "The Law of the Lid." As your leadership and management skills improve, so will the organization's. Ask yourself, "What can I do to improve my own skills to elevate the company?"

STEP 4: DON'T BE AFRAID OF HARD CONVERSATIONS

Delegation is a skill that requires having difficult conversations when expectations aren't met. To be effective, you need to react to missed deadlines or other deviations from expectations immediately. You can't wait. It's your job to find out why something isn't completed within the agreed upon timeframe. The conversation isn't about being right or wrong; it's about why expectations weren't met. I learned this lesson the hard way. If I didn't address a problem or concern immediately, something else suffered. The problems just got more complicated. My lesson was to nip the issue in the bud, and I saved myself and everyone else a lot of grief.

IMPLEMENTATION IDEA:

Set expectations to make hard conversations easier. Ask the employee to provide you updates so you know the status without having to track someone down. Delegating tasks means shifting responsibility to another person to be accountable for the results. If everyone knows there are repercussions for missed deadlines, the conversation shifts from blame to performance correction. Exceptional managers address issues when they occur.

Successful leaders know the value of delegation. They have a strong, clear vision, know what needs to be done, hire the right people, and manage to the outcome driven by their vision. It's not the act of delegating that we struggle with; it's the unrealistic expectation we have of the outcome.

Jeanne Coughlin, president of The Coughlin Group Inc., suggests four key considerations a CEO should evaluate before delegating:

1. A clear definition of the task or project
2. How you define success for this task or project
3. Decision-making authority—do you still want to be consulted?
4. The timeline for completion and your expectation for updates

Many business owners fear that by giving employees decision-making authority, they might make a decision that could cost the company money or even the loss of clients. They tend to get caught up in the never, never land of control vs. autonomy. Where do *you* draw the line?

As the owner and COO of a Stage 3 company back 1993, my confidence in delegating and willingness to release authority increased when I began to understand what I needed to focus on as a leader. Knowing what information to ask for, what to track, and identifying the key indicators were essential pieces to the puzzle.

I was forced to think in terms of what was good for the company; not what was easy or hard for me personally. If I, as a leader, couldn't effectively help people grow—if I wasn't able to admit what I didn't know or I was too concerned about being right all the time—there was more at stake than my ego.

When we moved from Stage 2 with 17 employees to Stage 3 with 22 employees, our revenue increased 55%. We had to accept the fact that we had outgrown our processes, outgrown our hiring practices and outgrown our ability to keep tabs on everything. We could either act like leaders and allow people to do what we hired them to do, or they would leave.

We brought in an outside facilitator to clarify our issues, keep the conversations positive and provide the structure we needed to move forward. The changes didn't happen overnight and a few people did leave, but we learned how to delegate and set and manage expectations. We went from Stage 3 with 27 employees to Stage 4 and 40 employees in four short years, and never looked back.

> *"Delegation is an issue of respect and how much we respect those that are under us on our team."*
> – Dr. Hans Finzel

Terry Barnhart, Principle of the Corporate College, shared this with me:

> *"Many of my clients avoid what needs to be done, because there is significant pain associated with the change of doing it. My chiropractor tells me that the pain associated with chiropractic care is the pain leaving the body as it adjusts to where it should be. Companies are organisms, and there is pain with change. Drucker's six rules to being an effective leader is a pathway to delegation."*

To paraphrase Peter Drucker—management consultant, educator, and author—follow his six, simple rules to embrace the art of delegation:

1. Ask what **needs** to be done
2. Ask what's **right** for the enterprise
3. Develop **action** plans and delegate
4. Take **responsibility** for communicating
5. Focus on **opportunities,** not problems
6. Think and say **We**, not I

WHAT AND WHY YOU SHOULD DELEGATE

"No person will make a great business who wants to do it all himself or get all the credit."
-Andrew Carnagie

Successful delegation relies, in part, on choosing the right tasks to delegate. I can hear you now, "But what can I really afford to let go of?" Meaning, I do everything so well, how could anyone else possibly do it better?

At some point in our company's growth cycle, I was so busy I had no choice but to hire an executive assistant. I was one of those people who was pretty sure I could handle everything and do it really well. Fortunately for me, my executive assistant was extremely good at telling me what I didn't need to do anymore. She helped me identify activities that didn't need my full attention. She taught me to identify the activity and then follow a simple process to decide what I needed to keep and what I could let go.

DELEGATE DON'T ABDICATE

In Stage 3, it's easy for a CEO who is overwhelmed by their newly discovered role of having to really manage people, to abdicate authority to anyone who seems to have a strong opinion or can talk a good story.

While you can no longer have your hand in everything, it doesn't mean you don't know what the company needs. Never, never assume someone knows more about your company than you do. No one.

They may know different things – have different skills – different experiences – but make no mistake about it. A CEO who has started their company from scratch and grown it to up to 34 employees knows a thing or two.

As a Stage 3 leader, it's your challenge to understand how to bring people into roles that will complement you and your skills and add value to the overall objectives of the business. Delegation is not abdication. A

> Never, never assume someone knows more about your company than you do.

business owner must become a great leader, and becoming a great leader makes the art of delegation a valuable tool, not something to ignore or rail against.

According to Jerry Houston, CEO and founder of HPI Solutions, "I think of delegating as similar to teaching your teenager to drive. It is necessary for you to sit in the passenger seat, no brake, no steering wheel, calmly providing direction and support, and being willing to accept that there might be a mistake that will cost you money!"

Dave Clough, who runs Power Advisors, recognizes that delegation is complicated and a lot of effort goes into doing it well. He says,

> *"Delegation is like a relay race where the handoff is critical. It is the one doing the handoff who is responsible for a clean exchange. If you let go too soon, you lose. If you hold on too long, you lose. In business, handing off before the recipient is ready is abdication; the CEO is too busy or doesn't care deeply about the task. Holding on too long is micromanagement; the CEO is not ready to let it go and trust the one taking it. The*

right balance makes for a clean handoff and leads to a successful and timely finish."

EXERCISE #1

Track all of the activities you do to run your business for four weeks. Each week, determine which of those activities only you can do and which of those activities someone else can do. If you have people in your organization who can step up and take on more responsibility, identify who they are. The first step to understanding how to delegate is knowing what should and shouldn't be delegated and why.

DELEGATION EXERCISE: WHAT CAN YOU DELEGATE?

STEP 1: IDENTIFY DAILY ACTIVITIES.

Commit to running this exercise for at least four weeks. Only then will you start to see a pattern in your activities.

STEP 2: IS IT YOU OR SOMEONE ELSE?

Once you have written down a week's worth of activities, complete the second column – ask yourself, "Is this something only I can do?" And if the answer is YES, put a **ME** beside that activity. If the answer is NO, then put a **NM**. (not me)

STEP 3: REVIEW WHAT THE INFORMATION IS TELLING YOU.

Here's where you have to take some time away from work. Find at least a half a day where you can FOCUS on the results of this exercise. What surprised you about this activity? What lessons did you learn?

STEP 4: DETERMINE WHO YOU CAN DELEGATE WHAT TO.

In the column where you had to identify if the activity had to be done by YOU or could be done by someone else, NOW determine who might be able to do those activities.

For instance, if you are doing all the finances for your business, could that be done by a bookkeeper?

If you have people in your organization that could step up and take on more responsibility, identify who in your organization could take on each activity.

ACTIVITY	ME OR NM	IF NOT YOU, WHO?

WHAT YOU SHOULD DELEGATE	WHAT YOU **NOT** SHOULD DELEGATE
1. Routine Tasks	1. Crises
2. Tasks Others Could Do Better	2. Ill-Defined Tasks
3. Tasks Others Might Enjoy	3. Confidential Matters
4. Tasks Good for Development	4. Praise or Reprimand
5. Time-Consuming Tasks	5. Planning the Development of Your Team
6. Tasks for Which You Are Not Responsible	6. Tasks for Which You Are Responsible

Ron Brewster, managing director for the worldwide nonprofit, Youth With a Mission (YWAM), believes, "Delegating effectively can bring ownership to employees. There is a big difference between renters and owners."

When delegation works, the benefits far outweigh the perceived disadvantages. The work required to create an environment where delegation is supported by accountability starts with a leader who understands the value people bring to their organization. It also starts with a leader who sets clear expectations and manages to those expectations.

BENEFITS FOR THE CEO

Lou Russell, Queen/CEO/Learning Facilitator of Russell/Martin Associates, has struggled with her own ability to delegate.

> *"I seem to delegate when in crisis and then find myself taking many things back. A leader's primary role is to develop future leaders and delegating is one way to grow aptitude. When delegating, you must carefully balance the quantity and risk versus the difficulty of the work. Help your employees grow by giving them small bits of responsibility at first and then more as they show the aptitude to do more."*

ACHIEVE MORE

Take the time to think about goals; not just the activities within your company. When my company was getting ready to move to a new office space, I had to delegate specific tasks to different employees, so I could keep watch over the bigger picture. Because moving is a time sensitive challenge, there was no way I could manage the entire move by myself, nor did I particularly want to.

I had to define what the tasks were, who could do them and how we would track our progress. I set up weekly meetings where my task leaders reported on their progress and I reported on the areas I was responsible for, so everyone knew how things were coming along. We always had the end goal and target move date in mind.

The day of the move went as smoothly as it could have. Because we had a plan, each person knew what their responsibilities were. We engaged everyone to have a hand in a successful move, and celebrated the new space with a pizza party.

GAIN TRUST

Delegating helps enhance your credibility as a leader. When you give your employees the opportunity to demonstrate responsibility, they give you their respect and loyalty in return. Learning to trust others helps your employees learn to trust themselves. Trust is an essential component of delegation, but it doesn't come easily for a lot business owners.

One of the main concerns I hear from leaders who struggle with delegating is, "How can I trust that Linda cares as much about this company as I do?" The short answer is, Linda will never care about your company as much as you do. But, a leader who communicates their vision and goals to employees, and helps each employee see the role they play in helping the organization achieve those goals, gains trust.

Nature abhors a vacuum. Leaders who don't share, who hold their ideas, their vision and their concerns close to their chest, leave employees questioning everything and operating more from fear. A leader who recognizes the value in strong, consistent communications, isn't afraid to delegate. Gaining trust becomes the reward for effective delegation.

BENEFITS FOR YOUR EMPLOYEES

"Don't tell people how to do things, tell them what to do and let them surprise you with their results."
– George S. Patton

Delegation positively affects everyone in your organization. Not only will you experience increased efficiency, but your employees will see the following benefits as well:

1. Personal Development
2. Self-esteem
3. Teamwork
4. Balance Workloads
5. Enhanced Communication

SECRETS TO EFFECTIVE DELEGATION

Want to engage employees and show them how much you appreciate them? Take the time to review the work that was delegated to them. Talk to your employees about what they did and why. Where did they come up with their approach? What obstacles did they encounter?

Vern Harnish, founder and CEO of the Gazelles organization and author of *The Rockefeller Habits*, reminds audiences that we've had the spoken word for 100,000 years, the written word for 5,000 and Excel spreadsheets for 50—so which activity do you think is more critical to long-term success?

Effective delegation requires solid communication skills to achieve the desired results. By managing demanding deadlines, empowering and equipping your team, and developing a second line of future leaders, you'll be well prepared to tackle the challenges inherent in Stage 3.

Always state the desired outcomes and results at the onset of assigning tasks. Explain what must be achieved, what the measurements will be, and clarify how you intend to evaluate the work. Ask what they understood and look for their reassurance that the task can be done. Address any gaps and reinforce your belief in the individuals. They need to know you trust them. Focus on results.

Concern yourself with what is accomplished, rather than detailing how the work should be done: your way is not necessarily the only, or even the best way. Allow them to use their own methods and processes. This facilitates success and trust. Empowerment is also about letting go so others can get going. Express confidence in their abilities and give them space to make some mistakes. Keep the communication process open to provide input, support and feedback.

> Explain what must be achieved, what the measurements will be, and clarify how you intend to evaluate the work.

Above all, effective delegation helps you manage your most challenging commodity – time: time for planning, strategizing, making decisions and sharpening the saw.

However, the responsibility of getting work done remains with the leader. If a task fails, you cannot point fingers at anyone. You delegated. It was your call. You may have picked the wrong person for the job. Don't throw the baby out with the bath water.

You must absorb the consequences of failure, create an environment where failure is an opportunity to learn and grow and continually improve.

"Hire people who are better than you are, then leave them to get on with it. Look for people who will aim for the remarkable, who will not settle for the routine."
– David Ogilvy

Challenge #1: Need to Have Better Staff Buy-In

Can you run a successful company if your employees don't buy-into your vision, your mission, or your core values? Can you run a successful company if your employees are content to just do their job, get their paycheck and go home? The answer is an unequivocal YES!

According to the most recent (at the time of publication) Gallup Poll on Employee Engagement, (2015) 71% of our employees are disengaged. That means that organizations have people roaming the halls spreading discontent and seeking to undermine their employer. While this is disturbing on many levels, the reality is companies run successfully every day. The bigger question is, how much *more* successful could they be if their employees were engaged?

In 2013, Gallup released its first *State of the Workplace* study, which revealed that only 30% of U.S. workers were fully engaged in their jobs. They have tracked companies that have gone on to launch well-intentioned missions, campaigns and strategies to reverse this trend. Despite these noble and seemingly effective efforts, employee engagement continues to decline. Our companies are being impacted by an epidemic that is totally curable.

Bad managers lead to disengaged employees. According to Gallup, "Engagement largely comes down to whether people have a manager who cares about them, grows them and appreciates them." In 2012, *Parade* magazine released a poll stating, "Fully 35% of U.S. employees reported that they would willingly forgo a substantial pay raise in exchange for seeing their direct supervisor fired." The data supports the assumption that most workplaces are toxic environments that make it impossible for employees to get excited about showing up every day.

> "Engagement largely comes down to whether people have a manager who cares about them, grows them and appreciates them." - Gallup

Jeffrey Pfeffer says in his book, *Leadership BS*, that the emphasis put on leadership has failed to create better leaders. He believes, "leadership training and development has become too much a form of lay preaching, telling people inspirational stories about heroic leaders and exceptional organizations." When, in fact, inspiration is a poor foundation on which to build substantive change.

The challenge of Staff Buy-in tends to focus on the manager. In Stage 3, the manager is usually the founder, the business owner and/or the CEO. In the exercises outlined here, we'll examine different ways to engage your employees and improve staff buy-in to transition into the next stage of growth. It's my goal to help you find opportunities to engage employees around effective activities and adapt the best-practices of successful organizations.

You don't need to be the best-trained leader or manager, but you do have to care about the people you hire. Period. If you care about your staff, they will teach you things you never knew and in turn, you'll help them become part of a winning team.

EXERCISE #1: CREATE YOUR VISION AND MISSION

If you have created your vision and mission for your company, congratulations! By Stage 3, you must articulate your vision to keep you and your team focused on where the company is going and how it's going to get there.

Brad Feld, founder and owner of the Foundry Group, has been an early stage investor and entrepreneur since 1987. According to Brad,

> *"Early on, especially pre- or early revenue, lack of focus is the death of so many companies. Sure, there's a point where you are still thrashing around looking for 'the thing.' But at some point you have to focus. What word do you own? Who is your customer? What are you selling them? How are you selling it? Why are they buying it? This is especially true when something is working. You'll feel like hedging your bets. But don't – go all in on the thing that is winning. Do it over and*

over again. And build scale quickly with it so that you can start experimenting with more things."

If your vision and mission are not clearly defined, you can easily get distracted by the "shiny objects" entrepreneurs are known for chasing. Knowing and understanding your core competencies allows you room for flexibility while staying focused on what you do better than anyone else.

A clear vision and mission helps your employees connect to the value of the company. With your guidance, show them that what they do every day drives the company toward realizing the vision. By understanding the mission—how you deliver on the vision—they understand what the company stands for, which shapes their behaviors and motivates them to succeed.

A vision statement answers the question, "Why are we here?" It communicates both the purpose and future of the organization. It should inspire employees to give their best and shape their understanding of why the company does what it does. The vision should remain intact, regardless of market changes, as it speaks to what the organization represents, not just what it does.

A vision is not just an idea; it is a force in people's hearts, a force of impressive power. Few, if any, forces in human affairs are as powerful as a well-articulated vision.

Keep your vision statement alive and visibly in front of you and all employees. Revisit it often and let it direct the company's actions and activities. This is the fun part: this

> Few, if any, forces in human affairs are as powerful as a well-articulated vision.

is where you get to dream big. Here are some questions to stimulate your imagination when creating your vision.

- What service(s) do you perform or product(s) do you sell?
- For whom? (If you have specific clients in mind, list them.)
- What are the keywords you use when describing your business to others?
- What are the words your clients use when describing you do to others?
- What does your business do better than any other?
- What are you known for?
- What is your unique selling proposition?
- What inspires you about your business?

Our vision statement is:

_____

_____

_____

_____

_____

_____

_____

_____

The business owner creates the vision statement. It's *your* vision; it's what drove you to start the company in the first place. While I encourage business owners to get input from employees, their vision is not what drives the company—yours does.

A vision statement has the power to transform the organization. It's a picture of what could be. It is a catalyst that can impel an organization to move toward a dream. A vision statement may also indicate how the organization will act.

Samples Vision Statements:

- "Our vision is to be a consumer centric company; to build a strong brand as a reliable supplier that our retail partners trust, along with market expertise and innovative product." Reseller
- "Trust us to light up your senses while we dim the lights, let the music play and bring the finest Italian cuisine to your table." New Restaurant
- "Our vision is to be earth's most customer-centric company; to build a place where people can come to find and discover anything they might want to buy online." Amazon
- "Become number one or two in every market we serve and revolutionize this company to have the strengths of a big company combined with the leanness and agility of a small company." GE
- "To become the Harvard of the West." Stanford University
- "To be the number one advocate in the world for human worth in organizations." Ken Blanchard Companies

In my opinion, the best vision statements are short, focused, clear, memorable, and easy to understand. The worst vision statements are the opposite: long, unfocused, unclear, easy to forget, and difficult to understand.

Vision is important for Stage 3 businesses because it forces you to pinpoint your ambitions. It declares the outcomes you expect and becomes a guiding light that will lead your business forward. When describing your business, which words trigger emotion? What jumps out at you? The words that inspire you belong in your vision statement.

A mission statement answers the question, "What do we do?" It defines the primary objectives of the company, refers to the present and leads to the future. It should include the organization's broad goals and how you will fulfill the vision. It helps your employees know what the company stands for and underscores the company values. When writing your mission statement, consider:

- Who do we serve?
- What do we care about?
- What will our customers receive?
- What is the desired result?
- What experience do we want our customers to have?
- What is our commitment to our customers? Our employees?
- How will we know when we have delivered on our mission?

The mission is a constant reminder to your employees of why the company exists. A meaningful mission can act as a moral compass and guide your company through good times and bad. It can help you make decisions that align with your values and goals.

A mission statement is a powerful, yet often underestimated, written tool for the small business owner. Not only is it an important foundational element in your business plan, it communicates your goals to your employees, stakeholders, and customers.

An effective mission statement considers the who, what, how and why of your business, and then whittles it down into a bite-size statement. Engage your employees by asking how they would answer the questions listed above. Their participation will help to solidify their buy-in to what the company stands for.

Our mission statement is:

_____

_____

_____

_____

_____

_____

_____

_____

Sample Mission Statements:

- "It is the mission of Sam's Design Studio to create unique and meaningful custom art home decoration pieces made from welded metal. Our goal is to make a customer's idea come to life through the creation of an art piece that incorporates the customer's personality."
- "The ASPCA Animal Behavior Center is dedicated to promoting balanced, respectful and enriched relations between people and pets through graduate and post-graduate programs for aspiring animal behaviorists; continuing behavioral education for shelter personnel, trainers, veterinarians, and other animal professionals; and the provision of practical, humane advice on pet behavior for owners."
- "The Children's Center's mission is to complement the service and education objectives of the university by providing education, care, and nurturing for the children of students, staff, faculty, and community members; utilizing culturally and developmentally appropriate practices; and serving as a role model of child care excellence for the community at large."
- "Our mission: to inspire and nurture the human spirit one person, one cup and one neighborhood at a time." Starbucks

A study by Bain & Company, the global management-consulting firm, revealed that organizations with clearly defined vision and mission statements, which are aligned with a strategic plan, outperform those without.

THE VALUE OF CREATING A VISION AND MISSION STATEMENT

Creating your company's vision and mission statement is not an easy task. Some business owners, who have their hands full with the everyday challenges of running a business, don't always make it a top priority. Some consider it a waste of time or something to put off until they are making more money.

To make this a priority, ask yourself: If my employees knew the potential of the business in the next two to three years, would they have better buy-in? If I can help them see how they fit into the larger view of what this company is capable of, would they be more motivated?

It took my partner and me a long time to create a vision for our marketing communications company. In hindsight, it was a huge mistake to wait so long. We talked everyday about our goals, where we thought the company could go, what it could do and how big we needed to be, but we didn't share that with our staff until late in our growth cycle. Because of that lack of vision and lack of mission, good people left when things became more challenging. We failed to show them the path we were on and how they fit into the journey.

This isn't the "nice to have" stuff; it's the must have stuff for anyone who wants their business to grow beyond their own view. It's fueled by the realization of the unique contribution your company has the potential to make and the lives it can touch. It clarifies your purpose, provides direction, and empowers people to perform beyond your resources.

EXERCISE #2: SET AND MANAGE EXPECTATIONS

Businesses everywhere across the nation are trying to cope with the lack of staff engagement. I ran a business with over 100 employees and I know it's a challenge to get staff buy-in, but it's not impossible. It doesn't necessarily take an incredibly talented leader or an exceptional manager; I know I wasn't. I definitely had my faults, but I genuinely cared deeply about every employee. I cared about who they were, how they felt, what they did, how they did it and why they did it.

I became better as a manager as a result of some lessons learned the hard way, such as:

- People can tell when you aren't really listening.
- They want to know what they are doing well, not just what they need to do better.
- People enjoy working hard when they know the WHY.
- When you take people for granted, they know it, and the good ones leave.
- I didn't have to know everything.
- I could trust people to do what they said they would do.
- How to communicate difficult messages and have hard conversations. How to let people go.
- How to accept my own faults and mistakes and own up to them.

When I began my career as a recreation leader for the City of Aurora, Colorado at 22, I didn't know anything about managing people. Recreation and leisure time activities were just becoming vogue. I was right out of college with a degree in Recreation and a minor in Business Administration. I remember my dad's comment when I graduated from the University of Northern Colorado in Greeley. He asked, "Are you going to teach people how to play?"

I was running a large recreation facility, and for the first time in my short career, ended up managing a large number of full-time and part-time people. When I look back upon my inexperience, I can easily spot my rampant mistakes. I thought my expectations were simple: here's what I need you to do. Go get it done. When something didn't go right, I was terrified to confront the person.

I remember the Director of the Parks and Recreation department, Bruce Waldo, gave me some pointers. He said if I didn't explain what my expectations were, down to the detail, when it needed to be done and how it needed to be done, I would always be disappointed. At one point, he taught me the proper way to run a vacuum. I remember feeling a bit put out, as I watched him run the vacuum. How hard could vacuuming be? He explained in detail why he ran it up and down over the same place to dislodge and capture the dirt. But the lesson took hold.

I learned how important it was to teach people the right way to do something and then let them do it. That simple lesson paid off in spades because I understood the importance of clarity through good direction, as well as setting expectations and then managing to those expectations. I went on to become a Recreation Supervisor for the City of Aurora, and helped build six more recreation centers.

Eventually, I moved on to become the Recreation Superintendent for the City of Loveland, Colorado in 1980.

Over the years, I've worked with many leaders and managers. The biggest challenge I ever faced was managing people. To improve staff buy-in and employee engagement, they must feel valued. You need to learn who your employees are and let them learn about you.

FOUR STEPS TO SETTING AND MANAGING EXPECTATIONS

STEP 1:

Meet individually with each employee in your company and find out what makes them tick. Everyone who works for you is a human being with needs, wants, challenges, successes and fears. Don't ignore anyone. Ask questions, and write down their answers.

- What do they like about working for your company?
- How do they feel about the work the company is doing?
- What opportunities do they see for themselves at your company?
- What are their goals, their desires, and their dreams?
- What changes would they make to be the kind of company they want to work for?
- Are they clear on how their own work impacts the company's products or services?
- Do they see the correlation between what they do and how the company makes money?

STEP 2:

Talk, *really talk*, to each and every employee. Listen, and listen well. You will gain invaluable insight that will benefit you now and into the future. After you've listened to your employee's aspirations, concerns, dreams and ideas, now it's your turn.

- Tell them what you worry about.
- Tell them how you got where you are today.
- Explain the biggest challenges you face as the company grows.
- Tell them what you are proud of.
- Tell them about the changes you feel the company will have to make to remain successful.
- Share your vision, revisit the mission and restate your core values.
- Explain your management philosophy and express your commitment to helping people enjoy their work.
- Let them know that you don't have all the answers, and you are doing your best to adapt to the changes facing the company.

If your company has more than twenty employees, you are starting to develop supervisory levels. Enlist your managers to conduct this exercise. Help the managers learn the power of listening and creating staff buy-in by being transparent and authentic.

STEP 3:

The value in Steps 1 and 2 pay off as you implement Step 3. Work with your employees to set performance goals and objectives. Identify the tasks that need to be done in order to deliver your product or service. Without the advantage of understanding your employees and your employees understanding you and what the company is working towards, this step won't be as effective. The work will likely get done, but you won't have engagement, which makes your job infinitely harder.

Start with the big picture and explain how their performance and their work impacts how the company will get where it needs to go. Employees want to know what value they bring to the table. This conversation is absent in almost all of the organizations I've worked with.

If you have a manufacturing company that produces a product, do your machinists understand how the efficiency of the production line impacts your ability to compete in a global market? Do they know who the competitors are?

If you run a service-based company, do your account or project managers understand why customer success is such a vital differentiator today? Are they encouraged to exceed customer expectations daily? Are they rewarded for doing so? Does the company celebrate small wins? If a client leaves, are the reasons examined openly and discussed with lessons learned as the outcome?

STEP 4:

Let's say you explained your expectations to an employee and they don't deliver. It happens. Stop feeling like a babysitter and start creating accountability in each employee. From the beginning, be sure to clearly communicate:

1. What needs to be done.
2. When it needs to be done.
3. What the consequences are if 1 and 2 aren't done.

Example:

Explain the **what**: We need to build 2,500 widgets

Explain the **when**: They need to be built in 45 days.

Explain the **consequences**: If we fail to deliver these widgets in 45 days, we won't get paid. Non-payment impacts our cash flow, which means we are not be able to make payroll.

Anyone hearing these three clear statements will not have a problem understanding what needs to be done, by when and why it's important. Then, why is it so hard for those widgets to be built and delivered on time? The deeper conversations don't occur. The smart questions aren't asked. Assumptions are made and not checked.

To be successful, manage the expectation you set. If Jerry's job is to set up the machines that will produce 2,500 widgets, he needs to know when to do it.

> You: When do you have to have those machines set up in order to produce the widgets on time?

Jerry: No later than 4 p.m. next Thursday.

You: Are there any obstacles that will prevent you from delivering on time? If you find any, please get back to me and let me know no later than Tuesday.

Then you need to make sure Jerry has communicated with you about any obstacles and verify that things are on target. Follow-up on your expectation by asking Jerry on Tuesday if there are any obstacles.

Let's assume Jerry doesn't report back to you. You find out that the machines weren't set up and production will be delayed a week. Now you need to have a corrective action conversation with Jerry.

You: Jerry, why didn't you have the machines set up in time as discussed? You indicated there weren't any obstacles and I expected the machines would be set up no later than 4 p.m. on Thursday. What happened? We've impacted our customer, which could impact our profits.

Listen for excuses and correct assumptions. Try to determine if there are real issues or problems and help to solve them. Is this a one-time issue with Jerry, or is it a recurring performance issue that needs to be addressed? If so, take the conversation to the next level and include the consequences Jerry will face if he doesn't step up his game.

ARE YOU BEING HELD HOSTAGE BY YOUR EMPLOYEES?

Rachel, who's been with your company for three years, runs a critical part of your operation. Recently she came to you, her manager, with concerns about overwork, working weekends, coming in extra early to get work done, lack of time with her family, and the pressure to keep up with the workload that seems to just get worse every week. She feels the company isn't operating from an organized plan, she can't hire more people because she is told that money is tight, and it seems her requests for help often falls on deaf ears.

Prior to hiring Rachel, you did the job she is now doing. You believe Rachel needs to manage her time better, quit taking so many breaks, and provide better direction to her employees. After all, when you were doing that job, you managed without any of the issues Rachel is complaining about. And you hate it when employees complain. You pay them well. Goodness knows, Rachel is making more money than your other managers, so why can't she just do the job you hired her to do?

The next time a work performance issue comes up, you let her know you are going to write her up and you expect her performance to improve. More and more issues crop up almost weekly, and production problems are now impacting the entire organization. However, things are so busy and Rachel is the only one that knows how to run her division. You don't want to upset her further for fear she will leave and then you'll really be in hot water. You're in a very competitive industry and finding someone to replace her will be almost impossible. Firing her isn't an option.

You continue to have conversations with her and try your best to hold her accountable. Time and time again, she falls back into her old habits, leaving her team frustrated and angry that she continues to get away with bad performance. You no longer trust that Rachel will do what needs to be done. She thinks your expectations are unrealistic and she's lost respect for you as her manager.

You are being held hostage by a poor performing employee and it is killing your company. How did you get here? Let's reverse engineer this situation and see how many opportunities existed for a different outcome.

The Issue: Rachel felt she was giving her all to the company and didn't feel appreciated for the hard work she put in.

The Solution: When employees are asked what the most important aspect of their job is, recognition is sited more often than pay or benefits. Simply listening and recognizing Rachel's concerns would have gone a long way toward helping this situation. Identifying two or three agreed upon solutions would have sent a positive message to Rachel that she was heard and more importantly, she was valued as an employee.

The Issue: Business owners who have been in charge of every aspect of their company since its inception can easily fall into the, "I used to do that job with one hand tied behind my back" syndrome. They have unrealistic expectations.

The Solution: Don't assume the job you did during the startup stage is the same. Growth is dynamic. What worked a year ago will not work today. As you move from CEO-centric to Enterprise-centric, hiring qualified people and providing them the support they need to do the job as they see it, is a critical step. This is about learning how to be an effective manager.

The Issue: No consequences means no accountability.

The Solution: Poor performance can be improved if:
1. The manager clearly outlines what the performance issues are, with recent examples, and explains what the consequences are if performance doesn't improve.
2. The manager follows-up and acknowledges improvements with positive support or addresses issues as soon as they occur and applies the consequences.

The Issue: Lack of foresight in planning for growth. There was no one who could run the division if Rachel left. Rachel was a great employee. She was frustrated by the lack of planning which she felt would have helped solve many of the issues she was facing. Poor management impacted her attitude.

The Solution: Part of a manager's job it to keep exceptional employees happy. The first step to holding onto great people, is to become a better manager. Employees need to be rewarded for great performance with recognition, profit sharing or bonus programs. Management should have encouraged Rachel to participate in planning for the growth of the company.

I believe every single person who joins a company has the intention of becoming a valuable member of the team. Their excitement level is high when employees start a new job. They're eager to learn, they want to excel and they believe they're making a good step in their own career path.

They want to prove themselves. They want to belong. They want to be recognized. They want to like their co-workers and be liked. They want to know the boss knows who they are. They want to be proud of the company they work for and they want their circle of family and friends to be proud of them for landing a new job.

Then, something happens that shakes their confidence. In many cases, that "something" is an inexperienced or simply bad manager. Your responsibility, as the CEO, is to ensure that your managers are skilled in growing and developing people. They must know how to set up systems that motivate people to deliver your products or services efficiently. Be proactive when it comes to managing the people issues in your organization because *people are your business.*

THE VALUE OF SETTING AND MANAGING EXPECTATIONS

Managing people isn't easy. That's because people aren't perfect, so working with them isn't going to be perfect either. However, ignoring your role as a manager by not setting clear expectations is a cop-out. All too often, we assume people just know what they should do, or we assume they know what we want them to do. Our employees are not mind readers; they need to be told what you expect, in detail. By setting and managing expectations, you'll get better results, you'll create better rapport with your staff and you'll increase staff buy-in.

RESOLVING THE CHALLENGE OF STAFF BUY-IN

The road to staff buy-in can be rocky, especially for the people who have been with you since the beginning. As you identify what skills and knowledge are needed to help the company grow, you begin to hire differently. You are now hiring based on specific skills and specializations.

People who have been with you from day one are apt to view the new, more experienced employees suspiciously. There is a tendency for people to trip over each other because responsibilities haven't been clearly defined. This causes a slowdown in productivity – felt first by your customers, who start to complain. The days of everyone doing everything are over.

The new hires bring experience and training and they expose the need for procedures and processes. People who have grown up in the more chaotic, family-like atmosphere will resist these changes. Staff buy-in begins to break down when new employees demand more structure, responsibility and authority. Without structure, the new staff will become frustrated. The lack of planning and undefined processes make it hard for them to buy-in to what your company stands for or where it is going.

The vision that you shared with those early employees has likely shifted, based on market realities and your customer's needs. This is a crucial time to revisit your vision for the company and help your staff understand the mission and why they are there.

Staff buy-in is the top challenge for Stage 3 for several reasons. The business owner has to let go and begin to help the company become less about them and more about the company. It's time to delegate more responsibility and authority, which means managing people.

Learn about your employees' goals. Find out what their strengths are. Ask for help from the people you have hired. Become more transparent and recognize that you don't have to have all the answers. Learn how to manage by setting expectations and then managing to those expectations. Effective management is the cornerstone to a great company. Your job as the CEO of a growing enterprise is to embrace these challenges.

STAFF BUY-IN QUIZ

Grab a piece of paper and see how well you answer the following questions.

- If you could improve specific management skills, what would you improve?
- How do you connect emotionally to your employees?
- Have you asked your employees lately if they know the value of their contribution?
- When setting expectations, what is your process for follow up to hold employees accountable?
- If you asked your employees today what the company believes in, what do you think they would say?
- How would your employees describe your company culture?
- What processes are in place to ensure you are aware of when your employees go "above and beyond"?

Challenge #2: Leadership/Staff Communication Gap

The most strategic planning tool a Stage 3 CEO can employ is bridging the gap between leaders and staff by doing one thing: *consistent communications.*

Start with a few questions to encourage on-going dialogue:

- What do your employees need from you?
- What do you need from each individual?
- How do people know they are successful?
- Do you know where the company is going?
- How can each person impact the bottom line?
- What makes a great employee?
- What is the culture you want to encourage?
- What are the critical conversations that need to happen every day?

Communication is a management issue, which is a new hat for a Stage 3 CEO to wear. According to researchers Marcus Buckingham and Curt Coffman, authors of *First Break All the Rules: What the World's Greatest Managers Do Differently*, "Good managers play checkers while great managers play chess. In checkers, the pieces all move in the same way, whereas in chess, the pieces move differently, allowing you to bring different strengths to the game."

Because many CEOs struggle to let go of control, they very quickly lose the support of their staff. The staff, who are working hard to exercise their own skills and to flex their independence, want the CEO to see that they are good at what they do. When their work is unrecognized, they begin to lose respect and trust in the CEO.

> Good managers play checkers while great managers play chess.

Think about it. If you have hired people based on their ability to do a specific job, but they are constantly second-guessed, or worse belittled, when they don't do something the way you think it should have been done, they will rebel. Or they will simply leave.

CEOs find themselves dealing with a staff rebellion in Stage 3. They will start to get pushback when they give direction; watch productivity lag; and experience higher than normal staff turnover. These are all symptoms of a company that is experiencing a Leadership/Staff Communication Gap. This gap will only widen if some critical changes aren't made quickly.

If you have ever worked for someone else, you know a "we/they" attitude exists whenever people are in a position to assert authority over others. This dynamic is hard to manage. It requires the ability to create a culture that rewards teamwork and collaboration, instead of control and power plays.

The CEO must be a good communicator. They must believe in their people. If that CEO respects the activity of management as a priority and hires experienced managers and/or trains star performers to be excellent managers, the gap will close. Ignore the activity of management and this issue can bring a company to its knees.

How do you know if there is a Leadership/Staff Communication Gap in your company? Look for these symptoms:

1. Responsibility is abdicated, instead of intentionally distributed, leaving people wondering what their job duties are.
2. Conflict runs rampant.
3. People argue instead of collaborate.
4. Good people leave.
5. People don't have a sense of how their work impacts the company.
6. Communications are spotty or non-existent, which leaves people to fill in the gaps.
7. Power plays go unchecked.
8. People aren't held accountable.
9. Leaders play favorites.

This challenge creeps up overnight. As a Stage 1 company, with 1 – 10 employees, it's very easy to communicate often and effectively with your employees. People often refer to their companies in this growth stage as a family.

When our marketing communications company was in its early stages of growth, we gave out bonuses in the form of shopping trips and nights out on the town. We had an all-female staff at the time, so shopping, seeing a play and having a great dinner fit all of us to a T! We really were one big happy family.

As we grew and added more employees, the gap between what leadership said and what employees heard widened. It became harder to maintain consistency in how employees were treated. It also became harder to have all the answers and keep everyone engaged. With up to 19 people to manage, the family atmosphere disintegrated. For instance, the employees who had started with us now felt threatened to some degree by the new people joining us. Why? Because those early Stage 1 employees were hired for fit not for specific skills.

As your company grows and delineates specific tasks, you need to start hiring for specialized skill sets. If those employees who joined you early aren't encouraged to keep up their own skill development, the company will outgrow them. It's easy to simply assume those dedicated and loyal early stage employees will continue to hold their own.

Changes must be made, and those changes often push business owners into areas where they aren't necessarily comfortable. Such as the necessity to have:

- "Difficult" conversations
- "Lack of performance" conversations
- "You need to move on" conversations

If leadership pulls back from these conversations, the communication gap will hinder growth. When my company was growing, we could no longer rely on the historical data banks of our trusted employees. We had to capture processes into manuals and impose those processes on our systems. It became necessary to create performance plans to reward employees with pay increases. The days of dropping $500 on a dinner as an incentive were over.

Systems begin to replace hands-on work that requires a lot of interaction. There is less opportunity for people to connect face-to-face, which only widens the gap between leadership and staff. A Stage 3 leader must take proactive steps to break down the barriers. The sooner you can minimize the communication gap, the more successful your company will be.

How does a leadership/staff communication gap impact your company?

- Low productivity
- Reduced efficiencies
- Increased rework
- High incidents of gossip
- Lack of commitment
- Customer service mistakes
- Project scope creep
- High turnover
- Finger pointing
- Blame placing

These are huge problems that can take a company down. People don't just become good managers overnight. They are taught. As the CEO of a Stage 3 company, you need to become good at managing people so that you can teach others to follow your lead.

Depending on your cash flow, you may even want to consider hiring a trained and experienced second-in-command to help you manage. Regardless, you have to set the stage for how your employees will engage and how your managers will lead, whether it's you or someone else doing the managing.

EXERCISE #1: THE ONE-ON-ONE

The one-on-one will, without a doubt, solve 90% of your leadership/staff communication gaps. I guarantee it.

As a manager, you need to spend 30 minutes a week with each of your direct reports. The goal behind these meetings is to open a dialogue. Notice I said dialogue, not a discussion about projects, or what work is being done or not being done. This meeting is about a manager connecting to an employee and an employee connecting to a manager on a deeper level.

This process will break down the barriers every time. Why? Because it's an opportunity for a manager to appear more human and it's an opportunity for an employee to express their goals and aspirations.

Benefits of the One-on-One:

- Establishes responsibility, accountability and proactive behavior throughout the company.
- Delivers and carries vital messaging between the manager and the employee that allows for clarity and truth.

- Provides consistent opportunities for one-on-one coaching, the most effective of all leadership styles.
- Demonstrates the importance of the employee's job/career development to the enterprise's welfare.
- Becomes the vehicle that allows the individual to self-correct unproductive and unsupportive behavior.
- Builds the personal commitment to high performance at a DNA level in every employee.
- Trains for leadership succession.
- Makes the continued execution of an organization's goals, strategies and plans a reality.

If meeting with employees on a regular basis has not been a part your thinking, start with small steps to establish the process as a welcome and engaging interaction.

In Vern Harnish's book, *Scaling Up: How a Few Company's Make it and Others Don't*, he shares how Google applied its data analytics capability, led by a "people analytics team," to bring the same level of rigor to people decisions as it does to engineering challenges. The data showed that periodic one-on-one coaching (as opposed to superior technical knowledge) ranked as the #1 key to being a successful leader.

1. Commit the Time: Select a fixed day and time to meet with each direct report and schedule the meetings six months in advance. Don't allow other pressing issues to derail the meeting. If for some reason you need to cancel the appointment, be sure to reschedule immediately so the process does not break down.

2. The First Meeting: This concept of the one-on-one is as new to the employee as it is to you, so make it a relaxed and open meeting. Suggested topics include:

- Introduce the intention behind the one-on-one. Let your employees know you are new to this. You are committed to providing an opportunity for productive dialogue on a regular basis (Once a week is ideal. Every two weeks is okay. Once a month is not effective.)
- Share your objectives for the one-on-one. Take them from this book and use your own words, or give the employee a handout with the objectives.
- Explain the time commitment. The first couple of meetings may take up to 45 minutes, but as you get more used to the agenda and the flow, they can be done in 30 minutes. (The point is to make them easy to handle and of solid quality, so you and the employee both get value.)
- Introduce key indicators for their area of responsibility. If you are talking with a project manager, ask them to come up with three key indicators they track on a regular basis that demonstrate the strength of their job performance.
- Explain that you are interested in knowing how they define success for their area of responsibility. How they perform in those key areas will give you a solid idea of their progress.
- Explain there may be other agenda items that either you or they bring to each meeting, but the time commitment needs to be respected for both of you.

Caution: These meetings are strictly about engaging the employee in meaningful dialogue regarding their progress. Be very clear that the employee can meet with you at other times to discuss difficult problems in more depth. If you allow your 30-minute, one-on-ones to become a two-hour discussion about how to solve the project management issue on XYZ property, you've lost the purpose behind the meeting. The one-on-ones are intended to open communication between you and your employee; they need to be protected for that purpose.

3. After the Meeting: Keep track of the things you talked about and the updates the employee gave you. How was their attitude and the interaction overall? Were they prepared? Were they confident and comfortable? Note follow-up areas for next time. Maximum time spent on this piece: 5 minutes. Don't write a book.

Sample dialogue promoting questions:

Adjust these to fit your culture and your environment.
- What is working for you? What isn't working?
- What do you suggest?
- Where do you need help?
- What did you do last week that you are proud of?
- What did you learn over the past week?
- What do you need to learn next week?
- How will you learn it?
- What did you accomplish over the past week?
- What will you accomplish going forward?
- How will you accomplish it?
- How can I help?

The employee will likely be reluctant to open up at first, but patience and persistence is the name of the game.

THE VALUE OF THE ONE-ON-ONE

The questions are designed to draw out how the employee is feeling about their job, their career, their goals and their dreams. Most managers are only comfortable asking job or project-related questions, but these dialogue promoting questions push buttons and forces the conversation to go deeper. Ultimately, the relationship will deepen too.

The intention of the one-on-one is to enhance the quality of communication between managers and employees. Once the employee understands how they add value to the company, performance and engagement improves.

EXERCISE #2: HOW TO ENSURE EMPLOYEE ENGAGEMENT

No business owner wants to feel like they are babysitting his employees. Those horrible closed-door meetings about behavior can be avoided. If you're thinking of shrinking your company back to 5 – 6 employees because the thought of more employees gives you nightmares, you aren't alone. However, if you plan on growing your business and ramping up, employees are a part of that equation.

Engagement starts with trust. It evolves into respect. And in time, the ability to improve the engagement level in your company leads to a better bottom line.

As a business owner, you have a lot riding on how your business performs. I know I felt that pressure when I was running a company with 100 employees. It sometimes seemed that every single employee simply came to work, grabbed their paycheck and asked for time off.

I believe that when people communicate, problems are solved, trust is maintained, no one feels taken advantage of, egos get stroked and ideas get generated. I witness good employees struggling to succeed. I witness good managers struggling to understand their employees. I witness the heartache when a good employee has no other option but to leave and I witness the stress when a good manager throws up his hands in frustration over an employee who won't listen. I also witness bad employees staying too long and bad managers creating a negative work environment that can erode any success a business has obtained.

ENGAGEMENT STARTS WITH TRUST

So, if you manage employees, listen up. Employees are human beings who have some basic needs. When those needs go unattended, the good ones leave and the bad ones stay. Both situations can take a good company down.

Jack, the owner of a small construction company for four years, recently received a phone call from one of his suppliers. During the conversation, Bill mentioned a conversation he'd had with Jack's employee, Larry, out in the field, in front of the owner of the project. Jack hung up from that call, walked into Larry's office and proceeded to rail on him about having that kind of conversation in front of an owner.

Jack didn't stop and ask Larry for his side of the conversation. He didn't call the owner to see if there was an issue or stop and ask if what the supplier had said was true. He didn't think about the 25 years of experience Larry had, nor did Jack stop and think about the countless hours Larry puts in for him every week. Jack didn't stop and think about the best way to bring up this issue. He simply reacted and he reacted badly.

In fact, the supplier had misled Jack. The context of the conversation wasn't out of line and Larry handled it with diplomacy. There was no issue with the owner of the project. But now there is an issue that Jack will be dealing with for a long time. Broken trust. And broken trust creates employee disengagement.

By simply taking the time to explore the situation and have a conversation with Larry, this very emotional situation could have had a much better outcome. That experienced, loyal employee is now questioning why he should stay. Over time, if this situation is left to fester, Larry will become one of the 71% actively disengaged employees.

Here are three steps you can take today to improve employee engagement at your company.

1. **Become a better leader**. According to John Maxwell's *The 21 Irrefutable Laws of Leadership,* "Leadership ability determines a person's level of effectiveness. The lower an individual's ability to lead, the lower the lid on her potential." In the example above, Jack's leadership lid is low and he eventually lost that loyal and experienced employee because he refused to address his own limitations. If you want your company to get better, you need to be better. In

Stage 3, the ability of the leader to paint the picture of what the company stands for and where the company is heading requires 60% of a leader's focus. The company is now enterprise-centric and those 20 – 34 employees, who are working long days and many weekends, need to believe in the dream. They need to be able to see how their job, what they do every day, brings value to the company. What are you doing every day to provide encouragement to your staff? What are you doing every day to provide the leadership your staff needs to stay focused and engaged?

2. **Learn how to have crucial conversations**. No one likes conflict, but as human beings conflict is in our nature. People have opinions, different values and different perspectives. So we aren't all going to get along every day. Bottled up tensions increase distance between two people. "I know what I said irritated John, but if I simply ignore it, he'll get over it." This type of internal conversation goes on in our employees every day. Your job is to make sure people feel comfortable having those tough conversations. Teach your employees that confrontation doesn't have to be an argument. Show them how to disagree with respect. Be the role model and encourage different opinions to show up in staff meetings, team meetings and company meetings. Encourage people to say what's on their mind and to think in terms of solutions, not just problems. Those are intentional steps a leader can

take every day to help employees embrace a culture of engagement.

3. **Be authentic.** You don't have to have all the answers all the time. When you aren't sure of something, admit it. Ask for advice. Set up situations where your employees can talk to you directly in relaxed settings. Join in lunchroom conversations. Invite people into your office and find out what they think about specific issues. Allowing people to see who you really are isn't a sign of weakness; it's a sign of strength and confidence. Find reasons to provide encouragement every time you have the opportunity. Your staff experiences growth pains with increased workload, unfamiliar processes, dealing with different personalities and staying focused on providing great customer service. Look for opportunities where you witness exceptional work and make it a point to say thanks individually and share successes in front of the entire team. When people see that you willingly look for opportunities to uncover positive progress, they will do the same. You'll help your team weather that Wind Tunnel we talked about earlier.

By starting with these three small steps, your employees will see you making the effort to be a better leader. They'll see that you address crucial conversations in a positive, respectful way. They'll see you as someone who isn't afraid to admit when you don't know something, and that you're willing to ask for help.

THE VALUE OF ENSURING EMPLOYEE ENGAGEMENT

I work with companies all the time who struggle with this very difficult issue. In many cases, not only are the employees disengaged, the business owner feels held hostage by them. In some industries, just finding qualified people can be a challenge, so if an employee's performance is less than stellar, the business owner is hesitant to address it for fear the employee will leave and they won't be able to find someone else to fill the spot. Now we have a negative chain reaction of events. Bad performance is ignored, other people see the lack of accountability and become resentful and soon the entire company is mired in a morale issue that is extremely difficult to resolve.

Never has the need for a strong and capable leader been greater. Don't let one bad apple poison the barrel. Employee engagement begins with you and trickles down to your direct reports. If your direct reports see you model the three steps outlined above, they'll follow your lead. With your encouragement, they'll continue to create a culture that helps people see the value they bring to the company.

> Employee engagement begins with you and trickles down to your direct reports.

EXERCISE #3: THE PERFORMANCE APPRAISAL SYSTEM

Nothing creates more tension between a manager and an employee than the dreaded performance appraisal meeting. If you've ever managed employees, you know the drill.

This meeting is when salary discussions occur. It's often when employees hear a litany of their shortcomings for the first time, some of which may have occurred months prior, leaving those employees frustrated and defensive. Unprepared managers try to find positive things to say to decrease the impact of the negative. It never works. All an employee hears when they walk away from those unproductive meetings is everything they ever did wrong. The positive is lost somewhere in their resentment, embarrassment and anger. There are so many things wrong with the typical performance appraisal system that I could write an entire chapter on it. This one evaluation system increases the leadership/staff communication gap in thousands of companies.

I'll give you some alternatives to the concept of the traditional performance reviews. I urge you to explore new performance management theories that make so much more sense than the old approach. I challenge you to start thinking about the system differently.

What is performance appraisal? The definition is "a formal management system that evaluates the quality of an individual's performance in an organization." Often performance appraisal meetings are a once-a-year event mandated by human resources. In the case of smaller companies, they're introduced by leaders or managers who remember their experience of performance appraisal systems and bring in something they are familiar with.

Your performance appraisal system should be unique to your company and support your culture. Don't allow the complexity of performance appraisal systems to deter you from making this a critical part of your employees' expectations. These meetings are paramount to your company's success.

1. PAINT THE BIGGER PICTURE

Because we are talking about this process as a Stage 3 company, the approach is unique to your size today. Your processes must grow as your company grows, so adjust accordingly.

As the CEO, it's your responsibility to set the goals for the organization. Your ability to define where the company is today and where you want it to be in 12 months determines how you will handle the performance planning sessions with your employees. Don't have this conversation in a vacuum. If you are on a calendar year, start early in October, and three months ahead if you are on a fiscal planning year.

Bring your employees together and help them understand the fundamentals of your business. Start small and make it meaningful to them.

Discuss:

- What your company stands for and your core values.
- Who your customers are and why they come to you.
- What your strengths are as an organization.
- What the company needs to do in order to make money.

- Explain what profit is and show examples of simplified financial statements.
- Help your employees connect the dots in terms of what they do every day and how they impact the bottom line.

How you evaluate your employees' performance has to start with where the company is going and how it's going to get there. Then, each employee needs to understand how what they do every day impacts those goals.

2. SET EXPECTATIONS AND PERFORMANCE GOALS

Start by identifying the critical indicators for your company, which are metrics that tell you when things are going well and when they aren't.

For instance, if you are a service-based company, critical indicators may be billable hours or utilization, the break-even rate, number of leads generated, revenue per employee, dollar value of proposals sent out, dollar value of contracts closed and work in progress. You may keep it simple and identify monthly revenue goals, monthly gross profit goals or net profit targets every month. If you are in manufacturing, you may look at sales goals, manufacturing costs, on-time delivery, cycle time, efficiency issues, inventory turn rates, customer rejects or returns.

It's your responsibility to engage your employees in a conversation that helps them see how each person's job impacts those key indicators. Once employees understand their key indicators and how they impact the company's overall indicators, you have a place to start regarding performance reviews. Now the conversation becomes: How are you performing against your key indicators this month?

By Stage 3, you should already have systems set up to generate reports and track critical information. Consider QuickBooks for financial tracking, Pipeline Deals for sales tracking or Salesforce for customer relationship management. These are simply suggestions for a starting point.

3. DETERMINE SALARY GOALS

As a Stage 3 company, you may have already put salary bands in place or clearly identified how an individual will earn more money. In the early stage of growth, salary raises are usually based on how well the company is doing financially, not how well the employee is performing. To begin the switch from what can quickly become a culture of entitlement (I deserve more money because of how many hours I put in) to a culture of responsibility (when I meet my performance goals, I'll see a 10% increase), you have to educate your employees on what financial responsibility looks like.

Financial literacy should be a requirement of all employees. If an employee feels they should make more money, but has no idea what they need to do to make that happen, the fault lies with the CEO, not the employee.

By using a profit plan (budget) to project your incoming revenues each month, your cost of goods and your general and overhead expenses, you'll be able to plan for salary increases. If you are running an annual payroll of $500,000 and expect to pay out salary increases on average of 15%, you'll need to budget an additional $6,200 a month to cover those increases.

How will you adjust your revenue goals to afford those payroll increases? Explain to your employees that salary increases are tied to the company's ability to generate more revenue. You are starting down the path of financial literacy by teaching your employees the realities of running a business.

4. MONTHLY PERFORMANCE SESSIONS DRIVEN BY EMPLOYEES

Set the expectation that it's your employees' responsibility to report how they are doing with their key indicators monthly. Work with them to create a reporting structure that is consistent and easy to maintain. The goal is to drive your employees toward being responsible for their own performance updates.

Train them to provide a summary report on any key indicators that are not in line with goals and have them offer ideas and suggestions on how to improve for the next month

Your role in these monthly meetings is to continually adjust employee's expectations regarding performance. Help them see the strengths that support their personal growth. If the employee expects a salary increase, there should be no surprises during the annual performance review if certain goals were not met or exceeded. This is not an annual conversation; it's an ongoing dialogue throughout the year.

5. THE ANNUAL PERFORMANCE CONVERSATION

In Exercise #1, you learned the process and the value of the one-on-one. With this process and the employee-driven monthly meetings in place, the annual performance review should be simply a review of how well the employee did overall and what salary increase they can expect based on their performance.

THE VALUE OF THE PERFORMANCE APPRAISAL SYSTEM

If you have up to 34 employees, you have started to delineate levels of responsibility in your company. Some of the weekly and monthly conversations may not involve you, as others may have taken on management responsibilities. Your role is to stay in touch with those supervisors and have them report to you how well their teams are doing.

Starting an on-going performance review mindset in this early stage of your company's growth will help align employees with your vision and ensure they are performing to your expectations. Open and frequent communication around personal goals and metrics help to facilitate the performance evaluation process and eliminates uncertainty.

RESOLVING THE CHALLENGE OF LEADERSHIP/STAFF COMMUNICATION GAP

My own development as a leader happened painfully. When I was the supervisor of one of the first and largest recreation centers in Colorado, I was very naïve and made a lot of mistakes. My approach with people was ineffective, at best, and often damaging. When interacting with my staff, I:

1. Treated them all the same. After all, I wanted them all to do the same thing.

2. Acted like I knew everything because to do otherwise would be akin to showing how little I really knew.

3. Got defensive if someone didn't respond to something I said and told them they were wrong.

4. Tried to get people to like me thinking that if they liked me, they'd do what I asked.

5. Ignored gossip thinking there's no way to really know where or how gossip starts and no one really listens to it anyway.

When I went back to school to study for my MBA, my approach to leadership changed overnight, thanks to a class that addressed the art and science of being a good leader. I continue to evolve and grow every day, because leadership skills don't just magically appear overnight.

A 2010 article by entrepreneur, venture capitalist and author, Ben Parr, said that Google used advanced algorithms to come up with this enticing and little known statistic:

> There have been 129,864,880 books published in all of modern history! Google defined a book as a "tome" – an idealized bound volume. Even if only 5% of these books are on leadership, there are over 6,000,000 books on the topic! Why then, is leadership in such short supply?

The answer is because, ultimately, no one can become a better leader unless they want to. Go ahead and read all those books by well-known authors and impress your friends and business acquaintances with the number of books in your library. Until you decide you want to improve your leadership skills, all of those books you bought are a waste of money.

Personally, I love books. I love reading fiction and nonfiction, and I confess: I don't read all business books cover to cover. I simply don't have the time. I do however, look over the Table of Contents, find a topic I want to know more about and flip over to that chapter. Then, I'm a maniac underlining, highlighting, making comments in the margins (this is why I always buy printed business books, never electronic). I'll even make notations about my clients next to a particular statement to share tidbits with them.

I read to learn and apply what I've learned to my business. For me, that requires taking in manageable amounts of data that are meaningful right then. Find books and authors that you enjoy learning from. Improve your own leadership skills so you can continue to help your employees become better leaders.

My go-to-leadership expert is John C. Maxwell. I've met Mr. Maxwell and found him to be as authentic as they come. In fact, I've taken his leadership certification program. He walks his talk and is totally committed to helping people become better leaders.

If you haven't found a favorite expert or book of your own yet, I highly recommend you pick up Maxwell's, *The 21 Irrefutable Laws of Leadership*, and start there. I wish someone had told me about that book when I was in the early stage of my career trying to be a leader and a manager. Unfortunately for me,

> Improve your own leadership skills so you can continue to help your employees become better leaders.

and the hundreds of employees I mentored and coached over the years, I only learned of Mr. Maxwell a short time ago. Funny. Here's someone who has written over 70 books on leadership and I never paid attention.

Several months ago, I received an endorsement on LinkedIn from Wayde, someone I had hired for a position in our marketing communications company. I hadn't heard from in 13 years and I was surprised and delighted. I quickly sent him an email back thanking him for reaching out and for the endorsement. Two days later I received this reply, "You know I think the world of you. You taught me what a leader should be and how a leader should act. Thank you for your example in my life."

That short, but impactful note helped me to realize that I had grown as a leader. The greatest compliment a leader can receive is to know they've made a difference in someone's life. Remember Maxwell's Law of the Lid: your leadership ability determines your level of effectiveness. Increase your leadership skills and your company will respond in subtle and meaningful ways.

Challenge #3: Need for an Improved Profit Design

In their landmark book, *Growing Pains: Transitioning from an Entrepreneurship to a Professionally Managed Firm*, Eric Flamholtz and Yyonne Randle outlined how a small organization navigates a tricky transition. Over time, the word "entrepreneurship" has come to be associated with an informal approach to management, or in some extreme cases, a total lack of management altogether. Many entrepreneurs think, "Hey, we got started without formal systems and processes, and we're successful, so we clearly do not need them."

People tend to associate processes with large corporations mired in bureaucracy. The association only reinforces the idea that systems and processes aren't helpful. Sometimes they can even be a detriment, which gives entrepreneurs a good argument for pushing back against formal procedures.

Flamholtz and Randle spend the majority of their book explaining and supporting the premise "that at some stage of growth, entrepreneurship is not sufficient and that the nature of the organization must change, together with the people that run it."

With the 7 Stages of Growth, we can pin down exactly **what** changes the organization needs to address, and **when**. My book series on each of the stages of growth, teaches you **how** to deal with those changes.

As a company moves from Stage 2 (11 – 19 employees) to Stage 3 (20 – 34 employees), it will experience an increase in revenues, profits, people and problems. Resources are stretched to the limit as increasing sales demand hiring more people, buying more equipment and caring for more customers. This is why Stage 3 is one of the more difficult stages of growth to navigate. The business owner must figure out how to scale the organization and move it beyond one person's area of control.

While business plans are well known, discussions around a company's profit design are few and far between. According to Adrian Slywotsky, author of *The Art of Profitability*, to succeed in business you have to have a genuine, honest-to-goodness interest in profitability. Understanding the underlying profit design of your company is critical to creating and sustaining a thriving business, and it's not just about the financial aspects of your company. So many people rely on data from a financial statement to evaluate their profitability, but they're missing the big picture.

Profit design is the result of managing and tracking a complex, interdependent set of components that contribute to the company's financial performance. Leaders must test all assumptions about different aspects of the business on a regular basis. The ability for a company to generate profit isn't just about making more money than it keeps.

EXERCISE #1: CREATE YOUR COMPANY'S PROFIT DESIGN

According to James Fischer, in his book *Navigating the Growth Curve*, "there are twelve critical elements that impact and determine the profit design of your company." In the following discussion about the twelve components of a profit, I'm going to suggest exercises to implement for each one. To help you identify where you feel your top strengths are, as well as areas that need to be improved, evaluate each question and generate discussion among your staff.

These discussion points may be potential areas of focus to help you improve your profitability. Identify where the company is doing well and find ways to capitalize on those strengths. Also, identify areas of concern and utilize all stakeholders in uncovering activities within those components that will improve profitability.

Grasping and utilizing the profit design components to your advantage does not imply that you have to hold all twelve of them in your control like a wizened chess master playing twelve chess matches blindfolded at one time. Quite the contrary; intentionally managing the twelve components of Profit Design is based on one word. FOCUS.

The talented business operators I've worked with over the years use the twelve components to focus their efforts where they are needed most. They do this by first, understanding the impact each component has on their operations and second, by intentionally setting in place strategic and tactical plans to address them.

Profit design creates the profit architecture of your company. If you are not probing into what is driving profits, revenue groups and motivating employees, you risk instability and going out of business.

A CEO who recognizes that the profitability of his company is based in all twelve of the profit design components, can build a company that will drive long-term and sustainable profits.

By focusing on the company's profit design, the CEO will stay ahead of challenges such as economic recessions or a major customer leaving. Building a solid base ensures stability even when the company faces issues that threaten its very existence.

1. Value Exchange: The examination of the profitable organization and exchange of value for money.

- Does your company effectively organize around its unique competencies rather than around a specific customer or key product group?

- Do you systematically forecast and track your company's key indicators by specific revenue groups?

- Do you track gross profit for each product/service by revenue group?

2. Customer Intelligence: The informed awareness of who the customer is and what they want.

- Is your company pushing products or creating customer solutions?

- Are you clear on who your customers are, as well as who they're not?

- Does your company carefully consider each customer contact point in the customer experience chain, in each revenue group?

- Are you extraordinarily clear about your customer profile in each revenue group?

3. Scope: The range and influence of products and services offered.

- Are you clear on what products or services you want to offer?

- Does your company have a narrow or wide scope of products or services that are aligned with your unique competencies?

- Does your horizontal or vertical product or service focus provide your company with a powerful advantage over competitors?

- Does your company's range of influence go beyond your current markets?

Wide Scope:

A steel business that sells steel products from rough generic steel, such as rebar and joists, all the way to selling refined, fabricated miniature steel parts used in satellites and medical technology.

Narrow Scope:

A steel business that only makes specialized 200-foot steel joists for the airplane hangar construction business.

Vertical Scope:

A steel business that owns the mill, forges steel out of iron ore, rolls it out into large sheets and has a cutting and stamping mill.

Horizontal Scope:

A steel company in the joist business that make joists for residential building, bridge building and boat building construction.

4. Business Development: The fusion of targeting, capturing and caring for the customer.

- Are you exceptionally good at targeting your marketing efforts to the right revenue group?

- Do you have a powerful, proven sales process for your sales staff for each revenue group?

- Does your company have a defined and effective customer service approach for each revenue group?

5. Strategic Control: The unique power of your offerings.

- What is the magnetic element that keeps your customers coming back?

- Does each revenue group have a significant barrier of entry blocking its closest competitor?

- Is your average customer's lifetime revenue value 20x the first sale?

6. Strategic Allies: The specific external partners engaged to expand sales.

- Do you have alliances that give you referrals for future business? (Piggyback alliance)

- Do you have alliances that equally partner with you to service your customers? (Symbiotic alliances)

- Do you have alliances that use your products/services with their customers? (Pass-thru alliances)

7. Knowledge Management: The manner and extent to which a company accesses and leverages its unique knowledge.

- Do you have a process that captures collaborative brainstorming sessions for on-going use?

- Do you have a system that captures company knowledge and organizes and stores that knowledge for easy access?

- Is there an effective updating process, so the latest information is available and out-of-date information archived?

8. Culture: The landscape and focus of the human workplace community.

- Is your company's cultural focus clearly defined and demonstrated by your staff?

- Are your company's core values defined and demonstrated by your staff?

- Are you confident that your company's invisible "out of earshot" culture does not manifest gossip?

9. Organizational Structure: The organizing of people to successfully complete tasks.

- Does your company utilize and leverage the talents and intelligence of your people?

- Does the leadership in the company intentionally plan for the firm's future staffing capacity needs?

- Does your company intentionally calibrate its performance based on the competency level of its staffing?

10. Operating Systems: The support structure for critical enterprise processes.

- Does your company intentionally research, design and plan for the introduction of new operating systems 6 – 12 months in the future?

- Do you rely on user feedback to improve your operating systems?

- Does your company effectively implement the introduction of new operating systems?

11. Research & Development: The continual discovery of solutions to your customers' needs.

- Does your company have a laser-like focus for the development of new products or services?

- Should you be shifting your mix from manufacturing to services and knowledge-based activities?

- Is your R&D department closely connected to the sales and customer service staff?

12. Capital Intensity: The measurement of required financial resources.

- Does your company have its capital investment fund requirements satisfied for the next 12 – 18 months?

- Do you choose a capital-intensive high fixed-cost operating system or a less capital-intensive flexible approach?

- Do your company's annual operating capital needs not exceed four months of top line revenue?

THE VALUE OF UNDERSTANDING YOUR PROFIT DESIGN

Remember the never-changing statistic that shows 80% of companies don't make it in the first five years? Chances are good they lost sight of how they made money, they weren't customer-centric in their thinking, they didn't explore their profit design and they didn't have a clear understanding of what drives both short and long-term profits.

According to Adrian Slywokski and David Morrison in their book, *The Profit Zone: How Strategic Business Design Will Lead You to Tomorrow's Profits*, there are three curses of growth.

1. High growth with bad profit design destroys value faster.
2. Besides being riskier, high growth is much harder to manage.
3. When a business grows by stretching its profit design to serve customers, the business design was not intended to serve.

By paying attention to how profit is created and being intentional about creating your own profit design, you'll not only improve your profitability, but you'll increase your business's value.

RESOLVING THE CHALLENGE OF A NEED FOR AN IMPROVED PROFIT DESIGN

Running a successful business relies on a leader to be very clear about where the business is doing well and where it isn't. Burying your head in the sand and hoping things will change is not an effective growth strategy. By looking at the twelve aspects of your company's profit design, you are forced to evaluate each one and not assume things are okay. You need to prove things are okay—not just to yourself, but to your managers, your bankers, and your investors. Having a twelve-point check list that provides everyone with clarity about what is working and what isn't working is a great start.

Most CEOs understand the need for a business plan – a road map that identifies where they are going and how they are going to get there. But many CEOs are not aware of the fundamental profit design of their business. This powerful tool should be considered before a business plan is ever introduced.

Start with having the profit design conversation with your managers. See how they perceive the twelve areas of profit design. Start a conversation. Help them build their confidence by under-standing the financial side of your business by talking about each of the twelve components.

UNCOVERING POCKETS OF PROFIT

"A profit design is the operative DNA of the organization, the interconnected guts of the enterprise. It provides a clear view of the core business, the adjacent business and the edge business. It is the customer intelligence, the pricing, volume and costing formula, the precise analysis of how you make and keep money."
– James Fischer, *Navigating the Growth Curve*

Focusing on the right things at the right time is what the 7 Stages of Growth enterprise model is all about. By completing the assessment on your company's profit design, you'll begin to better understand the relationship between all twelve components and start making and keeping more money.

Complete the Profit Design Assessment, and then, using a highlighter, fill in your scores on the Profit Design Map to see your strengths and your areas of improvement.

Note: The Profit Design concept was developed by James Fischer, author of *Navigating the Growth Curve*.

Profit Design Map

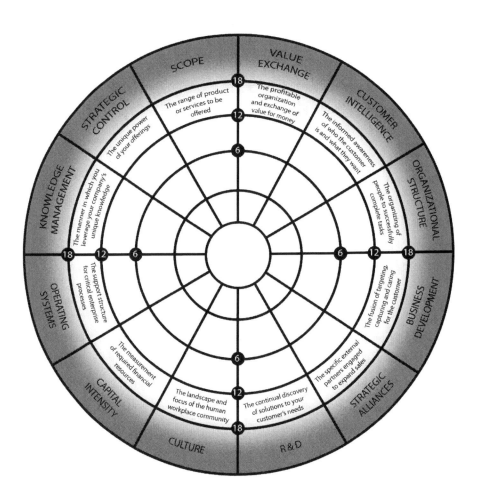

Profit Design Assessment

Directions: Please circle your very candid response to each of the questions below, indicating the strength of your agreement or disagreement with the statement.

Culture

	Strongly Disagree	Disagree	Slightly Disagree	Slightly Agree	Agree	Strongly Agree
1. Your firm's cultural focus is clearly defined and demonstrated by the staff	1	2	3	4	5	6
2. Your firm's core values are defined and demonstrated by the staff	1	2	3	4	5	6
3. Your firm's invisible "out of ear shot" culture does not manifest gossip	1	2	3	4	5	6
					TOTAL	

Capital Intensity

	Strongly Disagree	Disagree	Slightly Disagree	Slightly Agree	Agree	Strongly Agree
1. Your firm has its capital investment funds requirements completely satisfied for the next 12-18 months	1	2	3	4	5	6
2. Your firm has over engineered financial systems	1	2	3	4	5	6
3. Your firm's annual operating capital needs do not exceed four months of your top line revenue	1	2	3	4	5	6
					TOTAL	

Operating Systems

	Strongly Disagree	Disagree	Slightly Disagree	Slightly Agree	Agree	Strongly Agree
1. Your firm intentionally researches, designs and plans for the introduction of new operating systems 6-12 months in the future	1	2	3	4	5	6
2. Your firm heavily relies on "user feedback" to improve its operating systems	1	2	3	4	5	6
3. Your firm effectively implements the introduction of new operating systems	1	2	3	4	5	6
					TOTAL	

Knowledge Management

	Strongly Disagree	Disagree	Slightly Disagree	Slightly Agree	Agree	Strongly Agree
1. Your firm captures collaborative internal brainstorming sessions for later use	1	2	3	4	5	6
2. Your staff's company knowledge is organized and stored	1	2	3	4	5	6
3. There is easy access to your company's knowledge storage	1	2	3	4	5	6
					TOTAL	

Strategic Control

	Strongly Disagree	Disagree	Slightly Disagree	Slightly Agree	Agree	Strongly Agree
1. Each revenue group has a magnetic element that keeps its customers coming back regularly	1	2	3	4	5	6
2. Each revenue group has a significant barrier of entry blocking its closest competitor	1	2	3	4	5	6
3. Your "average customer's life time revenue" value is 20x+ the first sale	1	2	3	4	5	6
					TOTAL	

Scope

	Strongly Disagree	Disagree	Slightly Disagree	Slightly Agree	Agree	Strongly Agree
1. Your firm's narrow or wide scope of products/services is precisely aligned with your company's unique competency	1	2	3	4	5	6
2. Your firm's unique horizontal or vertical product focus provides you with a powerful advantage over your competitors	1	2	3	4	5	6
3. Your firm's range of influence goes beyond its current markets	1	2	3	4	5	6
					TOTAL	

Profit Design Assessment

Directions: Please circle your very candid response to each of the questions below, indicating the strength of your agreement or disagreement with the statement.

Value Exchange

	Strongly Disagree	Disagree	Slightly Disagree	Slightly Agree	Agree	Strongly Agree
1. Your firm effectively organizes around its **unique competencies** rather than around a specific customer or key product group	1	2	3	4	5	6
2. You systematically forecast and track your firm's key indicators by specific **revenue groups**	1	2	3	4	5	6
3. You systematically track **gross profit** for each product/service of each revenue group	1	2	3	4	5	6
					TOTAL	

Customer Intelligence

	Strongly Disagree	Disagree	Slightly Disagree	Slightly Agree	Agree	Strongly Agree
1. Your firm has an uncanny ability to **predict its customer's needs ahead of time**	1	2	3	4	5	6
2. Your firm has carefully considered each customer contact point in the **customer experience chain** within each revenue group	1	2	3	4	5	6
3. Your firm is extraordinarily clear about its **customer's detailed profile** within each revenue group	1	2	3	4	5	6
					TOTAL	

Organizational Structure

	Strongly Disagree	Disagree	Slightly Disagree	Slightly Agree	Agree	Strongly Agree
1. Your firm fully utilizes and **leverages the talents and intelligence of your people**	1	2	3	4	5	6
2. Leadership intentionally plans for the firm's future staffing **capacity needs**	1	2	3	4	5	6
3. Your firm intentionally calibrates its performance based on the **competency levels** of its staffing	1	2	3	4	5	6
					TOTAL	

Business Development

	Strongly Disagree	Disagree	Slightly Disagree	Slightly Agree	Agree	Strongly Agree
1. You are extremely adept at targeting your **marketing** efforts to the customer profiles in each revenue group	1	2	3	4	5	6
2. You have a powerful proven **sales process** being used by your sales staff for each revenue group	1	2	3	4	5	6
3. You have a defined effective **customer service** system for each revenue group	1	2	3	4	5	6
					TOTAL	

Strategic Alliances

	Strongly Disagree	Disagree	Slightly Disagree	Slightly Agree	Agree	Strongly Agree
1. You have alliances that give you **referrals** for future business	1	2	3	4	5	6
2. You have alliances that **equally partner** with you on customers	1	2	3	4	5	6
3. You have alliances that **use your services/products** with their customers	1	2	3	4	5	6
					TOTAL	

R+D (Research & Development)

	Strongly Disagree	Disagree	Slightly Disagree	Slightly Agree	Agree	Strongly Agree
1. Your firm has a **"laser like" project selection process** for the development of new product/services	1	2	3	4	5	6
2. Your firms new products/services are developed on an extremely **fast track**	1	2	3	4	5	6
3. Your R+D department is closely connected to the **sales and customer service staff**	1	2	3	4	5	6
					TOTAL	

Challenge #4: Unclear Values throughout the Organization

B eliefs create filters that develop patterns that drive behavior. If you understand this simple sentence, a world of knowledge opens up. Beliefs and values are developed early and are influenced by people, environment and experiences. According to sociologist, Morris Massey, we are not born with values. He defined three periods during which values are developed.

1.   The Imprint Period: Up to age 7, we are like sponges, absorbing everything around us, especially the ideas and beliefs that come from our parents.

2.   The Modeling Period: Between the ages of 8 and 13, we copy our parents and others, and we try certain ideas and beliefs on to see how they feel.

3. The Socialization Period: Between 13 and 21, we are largely influenced by our peers and outside influences. As we develop as individuals, we sometimes stray from earlier programming.

Values develop as we mature and help determine who we are as individuals. As the owner of a small business, your values help you make decisions about how you are going to behave, about who you will hire, and how you will treat your customers and employees. Without a defining set of values that each and every person buys into, behaviors go undefined, which leads to frustration and confusion and makes delegating even more challenging.

The business owner must define what values they believe are critical to the success of the company and share those values with every person they hire. When you're small, the values come from you. As you grow, values evolve and mature based on a collaborative work environment, shaped by the people you've hired. In a Stage 3 organization, the CEO plays a strong role in capturing and defining those shared values.

EXERCISE #1: IDENTIFY YOUR VALUES

If you haven't yet taken the time to articulate your company's core values, start now. I encourage business owners to identify what's important to them and write it down. What values drive the development of your business? How do you expect people to behave? Do your own behaviors support your core values? Be objective because you can't champion something you don't emulate.

Once you're clear on your own core values, take it a step further.

Ask yourself:

- How can I promote my core values throughout the organization?
- How can I recognize employees that demonstrate these core values?

Core values are the essential, non-negotiable tenets within the organization. They should be timeless and unchanging and help to define your company culture. They should define what drives employee priorities and how they should behave and think. They provide direction for all organizational plans.

Our core values are:

_____

_____

_____

_____

_____

_____

_____

□ How do you communicate your mission, vision and core values to your staff?

□ What are the benefits of every employee understanding these concepts?

□ How do you encourage your staff to provide feedback about the mission, vision and core values?

□ How can you encourage staff to "walk the talk" of the mission, vision and core values?

Core values capture the unique personality of your company. Start by talking to your employees and let them know how you define the values and what they mean to you. This isn't a one-time conversation. Use every chance you get to talk about these values.

Your core values help to define how people will and won't behave in your organization. They need to represent how you want people to act. Find out if your employees can site incidents where the values showed up during difficult situations. Help everyone understand why the values are so important in defining who you are as a business.

Business owners sometimes assume that everyone in their organization operates from the same set of values, whether stated or unstated. This common assumption can lead to a lot of frustration and disappointment. The organization's values must be identified and clearly articulated, so that your employees have a baseline reference point for their behavior. A company's values fuel the culture of your organization, and it's important that everyone understands, embraces and believes in what you stand for.

THE VALUE OF IDENTIFYING YOUR VALUES

I often hear CEOs say, "People just don't have good work ethic anymore." Specifically, they are frustrated by the Millennial attitude (the generation born between 1977 and 1992, according to Pew Research). The common perception of Millennials is "they just want everything handed to them," or "they don't want to work hard for anything."

People—no matter how old or young—are human beings first. It's human nature to want to understand the world around us and to find a way to fit in and be a part of something. Communication goes a long way toward finding common ground. It's your responsibility as the CEO to understand each individual and help them understand the value they bring to your organization. Don't assume they will catch on or simply get on board. You need to talk to them and explain how the values should drive their thinking. Stage 3 is a critical evolution for your organization. Educating every single person you hire on the company's core values is an excellent way to get a leg up.

EXERCISE #2: SELECTING YOUR CORE VALUES

There is a simple process that helps to articulate your core values. Restrict the number of values you have to 5 or 6, so people can remember them and use them in their daily activities. Your organization is likely already operating by a set of core values. They may simply need to be articulated and defined.

A company's values – what it stands for and what it believes in – are crucial to its competitive success. It's the *ideas* behind a business that encourage employees to care, not some manager with authority. The values must support the mission and vision of the organization. They should direct how people behave and help employees make better decisions.

Examine this list of values and add more as appropriate for your organization.

VALUES DEVELOPMENT EXERCISE

_____ ACHIEVEMENT	_____ HONESTY
_____ ADVENTURE	_____ HONOR
_____ ACCOUNTABILITY	_____ INTEGRITY
_____ APPRECIATION	_____ IMPROVEMENT
_____ ACCURACY	_____ INGENUITY
_____ BALANCE	_____ INNOVATION
_____ CREATIVITY	_____ IMAGINATION
_____ CANDOR	_____ INDEPENDENCE
_____ COLLABORATION	_____ JUDGMENT
_____ COOPERATION	_____ KNOWLEDGE
_____ COMMUNICATION	_____ LISTENING
_____ COMMUNITY	_____ LEARNING
_____ COMPETENCE	_____ LOYALTY
_____ COMPASSION	_____ PERSONAL
_____ COURAGE	DEVELOPMENT

____ COMMITMENT	____ PERSONAL COURAGE
____ CUSTOMER SERVICE	____ PROFITABILITY
____ CARING	____ PERFORMANCE
____ CHARACTER	____ POWER
____ DIVERSITY	____ QUALITY
____ DEMOCRACY	____ RECOGNITION
____ DECISIVENESS	____ RESPECT
____ DEDICATED	____ RISK TAKING
____ DISCIPLINE	____ RESPONSIBILITY
____ ETHICAL PRACTICES	____ RELATIONSHIPS
____ EXCELLENCE	____ SAFETY
____ EMPOWERMENT	____ SCIENCE
____ EDUCATION	____ SERVICE
____ FAMILY	____ STABILITY
____ FUN	____ STRONG WORK ETHIC
____ FRIENDSHIP	____ SELFLESS SERVICE
____ FAIRNESS	____ SECURITY
____ FINANCIAL SECURITY	____ STABILITY
____ FREEDOM	____ TOLERANCE
____ GROWTH	____ TRUST
____ HELPFULNESS	____ TRUTH
____ HEALTH	____ WEALTH
____ HUMILITY	____ WISDOM

THE 5-STEP PROCESS TO DEVELOPING COMPANY VALUES

Step 1: Distribute a list of values to your staff and ask each person to select the Top 10 values they feel represents your company today. Your personal core values must be on this list.

Step 2: Encourage your employees to add any values they feel are missing.

Step 3: Once everyone has submitted their list, set up a meeting to discuss. On a flip chart, write down all of the values that made it to the Top 10 list.

Step 4: Engage your employees in a dialogue about what each value means to them. Look for words that reappear and statements that are alike. Ask:

- What are you expecting from the company?
- How would the company be different if the values were more prominent and practiced?
- What are you willing to do to create a company in which these values are paramount?

Step 5: Ask everyone to circle their Top 5 values out of the 10, using different colored markers. The goal is to reach consensus by getting everyone to agree and align behind the final five values.

This is a fun and empowering exercise for everyone. As the facilitator, encourage conversations and make sure everyone in the room is being heard. Don't hesitate to bring in an outside expert to help you manage this important process. Sometimes an outside person is able to be more objective and can help to clarify which values really describe how the company operates. Once the core values have been selected, make sure you and your staff are living in honor of them every day.

THE VALUE OF SELECTING YOUR CORE VALUES

When we communicate with a language that everyone understands, we are much more successful in getting results. If you've ever tried to explain the last movie of a trilogy, you'll get heads nodding from the people who saw the first two movies and blank stares from the people who didn't. That's because the people who saw the first two movies have a shared language. It may be the names of the characters, or where the movie took place or the action in a particular scene, but they are connecting with you because of a shared language. Values create that language and help direct behaviors at the same time.

EXERCISE #3: CREATE A TRAINING PROGRAM AROUND YOUR VALUES

Another way to communicate the company's core values is through training. Consider implementing a core curriculum and training program to bring all new employees up to speed and give existing employees a refresher course.

Be clear about what behaviors are expected and what behaviors aren't tolerated. Relate everything back to the values of the company. Talk about how the company started, why you are passionate about what you do, who your best customers are, what makes a good fit when it comes to hiring employees and why.

Share the company's successes and failures, and explain how you learned from those failures. Let people know you, the CEO, make mistakes and that those mistakes ultimately lead to better decision-making. Model the behaviors you expect to see by being explicit about your own vulnerability and failings. The more open and honest you are, the more human you'll become in the eyes of your employees.

> Model the behaviors you expect to see by being explicit about your own vulnerability and failings.

THREE STEPS TO CREATING A VALUE-CENTERED COMPANY CULTURE:

1. Align the vision, strategies and operating procedures of your company with its unique culture and core values.

2. Design and manage key processes to ensure people are hired, retained, promoted and highly compensated according to your company's culture and values.

3. Provide evidence that promotes belief in the central importance of company values. This evidence is made up of values-consistent practices and goals as well as company lore, posters, prizes, awards and other tangible reminders.

THE VALUE OF CREATING A TRAINING PROGRAM AROUND YOUR VALUES

Stage 3 leaders must be intentional about every aspect of their company. When you create a culture that values training and directs resources to this critical activity, you will reduce the chaos and improve employee engagement. Your staff will be considerably more invested in what you stand for and they will know how to behave because your expectations have been clearly stated.

Clarity around how employees should behave dramatically reduces employee performance issues. Of course, just creating a list of values and posting them on the lunchroom wall isn't effective. Once those values are created, a company has to walk the talk.

The positive outcomes that derive from a values-driven company culture include:

Better decisions: When employees understand the company's values, they are better able to approach decisions by asking, "Is this decision in alignment with our company values? Which decision best represents us?" Even though employees may not make the same decision as the business owner, as long as their decision lines up with the values, you can rest easy knowing the outcome will be okay.

Better behaviors: When you define your values, you also define what behaviors you want and what behaviors you don't want. Once a definition is created and agreed upon by the entire organization, for example integrity, it is easy for a manager to explain to an employee why their behavior wasn't in line with the company's view of integrity.

Better performance: When employees are clear about how they need to behave, they can perform better. They don't have to question every decision or second-guess what and how they do things.

Improved culture: The outcome of the above all lead to a culture where employees are focused on doing the work that needs to be done in an atmosphere of support and collaboration.

The failure to develop and incorporate core values in your company causes confusion and hinders your organization's overall performance and growth potential.

Always ask yourself if your staff is operating in alignment with the values. When is the last time you talked about their importance? Go back to your training materials and revisit the topic frequently. Whenever performance issues come into play, return to the values. They are the foundation of the business and a key tool for team building.

RESOLVING THE CHALLENGE OF UNCLEAR VALUES THROUGHOUT THE ORGANIZATION

Well-defined core values are a must for a Stage 3 leader looking to delegate more responsibility and authority.

I've worked with many CEOs who have not taken the time to articulate their core values. When I ask what they believe their values are, they easily rattle several off: excellence, innovation, customer service, integrity, and collaboration. When they're pressed on how those values are represented in the company, I get a lot of blank looks. If I ask if the employees have been educated on the values, the answers are vague.

Introducing and articulating the core values of any company, no matter the size, helps drive the behaviors of each and every employee. So, if you don't have core values in place, you have work to do. Get your key employees involved in helping to create and define what they are and model the behaviors you expect to see. If this is done before a company reaches Stage 3, your world will be significantly more manageable. That's a guarantee.

Challenge #5:
Company Culture is
Resistant to Change

People fear the unknown, and as a result are generally resistant to change. It is in the best interest of every CEO to make sure there is a strong communication plan in place, to help ease some of the uncertainty that crops up in growing companies. A communication plan is simply a way of intentionally determining what needs to be communicated, to whom, when, how often and in what format. Resistance to change can unhinge a company, but it's also one of the easiest challenges to overcome.

Easy that is, if you are willing to communicate to the entire company what you are doing, thinking and yes, feeling. Err on the side of too much information, instead of trying to guess what you think people want to know.

CEOs typically view change much differently than the people who work for them, because they have the benefit of a 360-degree view. So, tell them what you see, and how they will be impacted. Lay out the short and long-term implications of the changes they are experiences and share how the issues will be resolved. Get ahead of the story by being completely upfront and transparent.

Earlier we talked about a "hidden agent" known as the Builder/ Protector Ratio. Builders love risk, aren't afraid of change, seek out opportunities and are always looking for the next challenge (sounds like the owner, right?). Protectors are risk averse, suspicious of growth and uncomfortable with change. Companies need both to be successful.

> Get ahead of the story by being completely upfront and transparent.

If you adopt a Protector mindset when change occurs, you will send a wave of fear throughout the organization, which causes people to shut down. Instead, you must embrace the Builder mindset and be an agent for change, because change is essential for growth. When you are confident in the face of change, your employees will be less resistant. By effectively managing employees' expectations of growth, you will make change easier for them to swallow and less terrifying. Developing a culture that embraces change requires a CEO who is intentional in communicating all aspects of what the company is going through.

The world is changing. Some economists predict that we will never go back to the economic baseline we were operating at before the great recession. This means expectations have to change. Perceptions of growth need to adapt to the new economy. Certain activities (downsizing, reengineering, outsourcing and re-strategizing) that companies struggled to deal with as a result of economic changes in the past several years will likely become the new norm.

Companies must create cultures that embraces change, not as a reaction, but as a business objective – a strategy similar to planning for revenue growth. A plan for change should be included in every manager's performance planning process. Employees should be trained to expect things to change and be a part of the process. By creating a change mindset, CEOs can improve staff buy-in and reduce dissent. This helps minimize the uncertainty that fear creates, which can impact a company's ability to stay ahead of competitors.

EXERCISE #1: IDENTIFY THE CHANGE: WHAT IS HAPPENING AND WHY?

First, identify what is happening and take the time to explain why it's happening. It is the CEO's job to communicate what is changing and why. When you run a company, you expect things to change. In fact, you are the harbinger of change and see it as your responsibility to keep the organization fresh, performing ahead of the competition and profitable. You are in control of most of the change that happens. Your employees see change as something that happens to them and something they have no control over.

Share with the entire staff what is changing, why it is changing and the benefits of the change. Then, get everyone's input on how they will be impacted by the new process, the new office space, a new or additional product line, changes to the organizational chart, policy or whatever it is.

THE VALUE OF IDENTIFYING CHANGE

In John P. Kotter's popular book, *Leading Change,* he identifies eight mistakes that hinder change efforts. His also provides eight strategies to manifest sustainable change within an organization. The first step starts with establishing a sense of urgency around the event. This supports my premise that you have to communicate the why behind the change and create the urgency that Kotter refers to.

8 COMMON MISTAKES THAT SABOTAGE CHANGE

1. Allowing too much complacency
2. Failing to create a sufficiently powerful guiding coalition
3. Underestimating the power of vision
4. Undercommunicating the vision by a factor of 10 (or 100 or even 1,000)
5. Permitting obstacles to block the new vision
6. Failing to create short-term wins
7. Declaring victory too soon
8. Neglecting to anchor changes firmly in the culture

8 STEPS OF CREATING MAJOR CHANGE

1. Establishing a sense of urgency
2. Creating a guiding coalition
3. Developing a vision and strategy
4. Communicating the change vision
5. Empowering broad-based action
6. Generating short-term wins

7. Consolidating gains and producing more change
8. Anchoring new approaches in the culture

EXERCISE #2: DEVELOP A STRATEGY TO COPE WITH CHANGE

Often, business owners simply decide on a specific course of action and expect their team to happily accept the decision and go along with whatever has been decided. This happens frequently in small businesses, where the CEO is accustomed to making all of the decisions, calling all the shots, bringing in all of the sales, and generally handling all aspects of running the company. He may not see process changes, hiring decisions, or product offerings as a big deal. They are clear about how that change fits into the larger vision of where the company is going. Not so with the employees. Their world is already reeling from the last decision the CEO made. While they may go along with the latest decision, resentment is building.

The ability of a leader to move from a Stage 2, CEO-centric company to a Stage 3, Enterprise-centric company has everything to do with sharing their vision and the strategy behind their decisions. It's not an easy switch to make, particularly for someone who is used to calling all the shots and making things happen.

When a leader can clearly explain why they are making the decision and what changes will occur as a result, they'll experience better overall buy-in. Define the vision for the new initiative and help each person understand the strategy behind the change. Just because you believe the change is right for the company, doesn't mean your employees will. But when they understand your strategy and your thought process, they'll be more apt to accept the change.

> Define the vision for the new initiative and help each person understand the strategy behind the change.

If your employees are resistant to change, it's because they don't understand how they will be impacted and they assume the worst. Help them to understand by articulating the reason for the change and how it will help the company improve profitability, productivity or performance. Take the time to talk with each person individually, so they can ask questions about how their job will be affected. People need to have a chance to share their opinions, to talk things out and to voice concerns.

Listen not only to what's being said, but also to what isn't being said. If someone appears to be unhappy with your decision, but won't come out and say so, ask the tough questions that will bring them closer to expressing themselves. Don't expect people to open up and tell you what they are thinking or feeling. They fear reprisal, or worse, being seen as negative or inflexible. It's your responsibility to open up the lines of communication and let people know you appreciate and welcome their thoughts and their concerns.

THE VALUE OF DEVELOPING A STRATEGY TO COPE WITH CHANGE

In his book, *Heart of Change*, John Kotter says, "Changing behavior is less a matter of giving people analysis to influence their thoughts than helping them to see a truth to influence their feelings." By helping people understand the purpose of change, how it will impact them, and how they can help make the change successful, you are appealing to their emotions. Emotions are powerful change agents. Encourage discussions about how things "used to be" and what can be. Help people get behind the vision of what that change initiative will look like when it's complete. How will things be different and why?

Change will always be a part of your business. Take the time to create a culture where change is perceived as exciting, fun and rewarding.

EXERCISE #3: BE PREPARED FOR RESISTANCE

Next, deal with the (inevitable) resistance in a proactive and positive manner. If you find that people are unwilling to embrace the new initiative and there are a lot of rumors floating around, you need to bring everyone together quickly, address those rumors and solicit support.

Dealing with change, as difficult as it can be in Stage 3, isn't nearly as difficult as when you have over 100 employees. In this stage, you have the ability to help each person understand the need for change and more importantly, how that change will impact them directly. People will embrace what they understand. They will sabotage your efforts if they think the initiative is wrongheaded or unnecessary. Your job is to show how the change will enhance the overall good of the company and ultimately every person in the company.

In your one-on-ones with your direct reports, find out how they are being impacted by change and ask how they are dealing with it. As with so many critical issues in organiza-

> People will embrace what they understand.

tions, it's so easy to ignore this basic approach. Ask what they have observed about their own behavior and others. Start the dialogue about what they are experiencing with their own job responsibilities when it comes to change initiatives.

When you hear someone complain about a new process or the addition of a new employee or a new piece of equipment, don't ignore it. Address the issue immediately. Off-handed negative remarks have the power to derail any type of change initiative. A manager who allows those negative remarks to go unchallenged may think it's just an isolated attitude, but more than likely, those same remarks are being repeated out of earshot to anyone who will listen. Negativity has a way of taking on a life of its own, so nip it in the bud, before it permeates the culture.

THE VALUE OF BEING PREPARED FOR RESISTANCE

Sometimes the reason our change efforts don't stick is we allow people to damage those efforts without any consequence. If you are a leader who deals well with conflict, you'll address the issue straight on, work to understand the cause of the conflict and find ways to minimize that conflict. You'll be a better change catalyst than someone who shies away from conflict.

Conflict management and resolution is a critical competency for a Stage 3 leader. Change always brings conflict, but a strong leader knows how to deal with people who are not happy, who are disgruntled, or who play games and spread rumors. When you learn how to handle conflict, resistance will be easier to manage.

RESOLVING THE CHALLENGE OF A CULTURE RESISTANT TO CHANGE

Culture can be defined as the shared patterns of behaviors and interactions, cognitive constructs, and affective understanding that are learned through a process of socialization.

What behaviors do you accept? What behaviors won't you accept? How do you educate your employees on what you care about as an organization? Never doubt that your employees want to know how they should behave, how they should act, and what is acceptable or not acceptable behaviors and attitudes. Don't hesitate to drill down into how group behaviors impact your company. Explain what you care about and what got you to where you are today. Your stories are important. Your values are critical.

I was conducting an exit interview with a short-term employee one time and asked why they were leaving. I had high expectations for this person and was sad to see that after only 11 months, they were moving on. I really wanted to understand this person's decision.

The answer was hard to hear. "There are too many cliques in your company. It's almost impossible for someone new to come in and feel a part of the company. I never felt accepted or understood what it would take to become a part of your culture." Ouch.

When you look at your organization and think about change as it relates to your culture, remember culture isn't an organizational issue; it's a personal issue. It is how each and every person in your organization reacts to different circumstances.

Clearly, we had ignored how the group culture was impacting individuals. We talked about our culture and our values and we gave examples of how proud we were of that culture. However, we never really examined how that culture showed up internally, especially when it came to bringing on new employees. I was angry that we had cliques that discouraged newcomers from feeling a part of our company. I was angry that I had overlooked a pervasive internal culture and I was angry that a good person was leaving because we allowed that behavior to persist.

Help your employees understand that change is a part of being in business. Change includes bringing on new talent. Be aware of how new employees are treated. Be aware that subtle rebellions may be taking place throughout your organization. You may need to dig a bit deeper to uncover them. Ask more pertinent questions to get to the bottom of critical issues.

Fundamentally, we all know that change is inevitable. Intentionally talking about change and intentionally encouraging people to identify what change looks like is an on-going responsibility of any leader. How can you help a new employee feel a part of your culture? Can you explain what your culture is? Can you show examples of how your values have helped to define that culture? When your customers talk about your company, what do they say? Don't use culture as a flag you wave i.e. "Our culture is driven by our values." Use culture as a defining principle of how you expect people to behave and start to create a culture that embraces change.

What's Next?

The great thing about understanding your challenges upfront is that you can work on them immediately and move on! You don't have to worry about where to devote your time and you have a clear outline of how to move your company from Stage 3 with 20 - 34 employees to Stage 4 with 35 - 57 employees. As a leader of a Stage 3 organization, you are still in the beginning stages of navigating your own growth curve.

Business owners who have the ability to focus on the right things at the right time build successful businesses. If you make sure that you are working on these five challenges every day, your company will respond and reward you with results.

Many business owners are not able to put words to their issues. They simply know there are issues hitting them every day and they *react* to each issue separately, depending upon how critical the issue is at that exact day and hour. Reacting to issues is not an effective way to grow a business. Understanding your key issues, identifying them and working on them is a formula for success!

As a company grows, so must the leader. Each stage of growth will require something different. Understanding what is required of you as your company evolves can either propel the company forward or cause the company to stagnate: profits never materialize, sales suffer and there is high employee turnover.

> As a company grows, so must the leader.

"Letting go to let it grow" is the name of the game in a Stage 3 company. As you move closer to Stage 4 (35 – 57 employees) the priority shifts to managing your managers. Stage 4 is about hiring and training capable managers and having them help you develop people and processes in order to scale the business.

Are you ready to tackle the Stage 4 Challenges? My book, *Managing the Managers: How to Escalate Growth through People and Processes with 35-57 Employees,* offers tips on how to address the top five challenges for the fourth stage of growth. The bottomline in understanding the 7 Stages of Growth is that the complexity of an organization will always extract its due.

Take a look at our website, www.igniteyourbiz, for additional products and services for business owners who are passionate about turning their growing business into a great business.

> The complexity of an organization will always extract its due.

FOUNDATION BUILDING BLOCKS FOR A STAGE 3 COMPANY WITH 20 – 34 EMPLOYEES

Stage 3 brings a new set of challenges to the table. Here is a quick look at what you may be experiencing.

AREA	DESCRIPTION
Employees	You have 20 to 34 employees
CEO/Founder	You now find yourself having to manage people more than being the specialist you used to be. The fun of growing the business that you previously enjoyed might be fading as you encounter more and more "people problems." You are probably experiencing some entrepreneurial burnout.
Team	You have 3 to 5 managers. You have a team that is trying to gain more autonomy in order to assert their own expertise. They might be revolting or threatening to revolt. You are probably experiencing the pain of not wanting to let faithful employees go who no longer fit.
Business Model	You are using a successful business model but you continue to explore other market opportunities.
Climate	There is a lot of: (a) confusion due to lack of company-wide clarity on who is responsible for what; (b) who has authority for what; and (c) tension in the air as you and the organization are being stretched.
Systems	Routines and systems are still evolving and a bit in flux. They are not yet set in stone or well documented.
Cash	Cash is tight, as working capital needs grow from increased sales volume (A/R, Inventory increases) and payroll.
Focus	It is all about trying to keep your arms around the business while you let go of more responsibilities.

A STAGE 3 COMPANY AT A GLANCE

ENTERPRISE-CENTRIC

Number of Employees	20 - 34
Number of Managers	3-5
Number of Executives	1
Builder/Protector Ratio	1:1
Three Gates of Focus	People
	Profit/Revenue
	Process
3 Faces of a Leader	Visionary 10%
	Manager 60%
	Specialist 30%
Leadership Style	Primary – Coaching
	Secondary – Democratic
	Auxiliary – Pacesetting
Leadership Competencies	Accurate self-assessment
	Achievement
	Developing others
	Conflict management
	Teamwork and Collaboration
Critical Processes for Stage 3	Human resources
	Work community
Critical Activities for Stage 3	Profit plan is set up
	Defining roles and responsibilities
	More emphasis on accountability

ARE YOU READY FOR STAGE 4 - PROFESSIONAL?

The 7 Stages of Growth has helped thousands of business owners focus on the right things at the right time. The framework helps business owners to uncover the root cause of an issue and then resolve that issue quickly.

As challenging as it was to move from Stage 2 to Stage 3, moving from Stage 3 to Stage 4 requires the leader to truly put their money where their mouth is. This stage of growth is called "Professional." It will be the first time a CEO will see capable managers require higher salaries and demand even greater autonomy. You will be required to bring a whole new set of knowledge and procedures to the company.

Your top challenge in Stage 4 is Project Management and Resource Allocation and your top gate of focus is Process. Your challenges are mostly process-focused. If you aren't prepared to take on a much more visible management role, you'll need to find someone who can.

Your role now as CEO with 35 – 57 employees is all about your ability to take what you have learned as the CEO of a growing organization and help your managers incorporate their knowledge with your knowledge in order to capitalize upon both. This requires you to up the ante on your leadership skills and embrace the freedom that you will feel when those capable managers are helping you take the company to the next stage of growth.

You can order any of Laurie's books on the Stages of Growth at Amazon.com.

Survive and Thrive:
How to Unlock Profits in a Startup with 1-10 Employees

Sales Ramp Up:
How to Kick Start Performance and Adapt to
Chaos with 11-19 Employees

The Art of Delegation:
How to Effectively Let Go to Grow with 20-34 Employees

Managing the Managers:
How to Escalate Growth through People and Processes
with 35-57 Employees

ADDITIONAL RESOURCES

Bossidy, Larry: *Execution: The Art of Getting Things Done*

Buckingham, Marcus and Coffman, Curt: *First Break All the Rules*

Dotlich, David and Cairo, Peter: *Why CEOs Fail*

Feld, Brad: *Startup Life: Surviving and Thriving in a Relationship with an Entrepreneur*

Fischer, James: *Navigating the Growth Curve: 9 Fundamentals that Build a Profit-Driven, People-Centered, Growth-Smart Company*

Flamholtz, Eric G. and Randle, Yvonne: *Growing Pains: Transitioning from an Entrepreneurship to a Professionally Managed Firm*

Fleury, Robert: *The Small Business Survival Guide*

Goleman, Daniel; Boyatzis, Richard and McKee, Annie: *Primal Leadership: Realizing the Power of Emotional Intelligence*

Harnish, Verne: *Mastering the Rockefeller Habits; Scaling Up: How a Few Companies Make It and Why the Rest Don't*

Helfert, Erich: *Techniques of Financial Analysis: A Guide to Value Creation*

Kotter, John: *Leading Change; Heart of Change*

Ludy, Perry: *Profit Building: Cutting Costs without Cutting People*

Maxwell, John C.: *21 Irrefutable Laws of Leadership*

Pfeffer, Jeffery: *Leadership BS: Fixing Workplaces and Careers One Truth at a Time*

Price, Ron and Randy Lisk: *The Complete Leader*

Sinek, Simon: *Start with Why*

Slywotsky, Adrian: *The Profit Zone; The Art of Profitability*

Stack, Jack: *A Stake in the Outcome*

Tatum, Doug: *No Man's Land*

Weiner, Eric: *Geography of Genius*

HIRE LAURIE AS A SPEAKER

Laurie Taylor has spoken to thousands of business audiences. Her topics include organizational growth, using the 7 Stages of Growth as a foundation, leadership development and employee engagement.

CRACKING THE CODE TO YOUR COMPANY'S GROWTH

Challenging insights into how companies grow based on a unique research study that shows the complexity level increases as you add people. Knowing your stage of growth provides predictability about growing a business that you can't find anywhere else.

YOUR PEOPLE ARE YOUR BUSINESS

The biggest challenge we face as business owners is the management of people. We all know people leave managers, not companies.

If you address the reality that "your people are your business" early on in your company's life cycle, managing profitability, performance and productivity will be easier. Learn how to break down barriers that exist between managers and employees and create relationships that engage and encourage employees to excel.

EVERYTHING RISES AND FALLS ON LEADERSHIP

Who are the leaders in your organization? Is leadership improvement an intentional part of your company's culture? John Maxwell, the voice of leadership and author of over 70 books on the subject, identified five levels of leadership – Position, Permission, Production,

People Development and Pinnacle. Learn how to apply these principles and extend your own influence as a leader to build a culture of responsibility and authenticity.

You can reach Laurie at laurie@igniteyourbiz.com.

LAURIE'S CLIENT TESTIMONIALS:

"No one knows small business in America like Laurie. There is not one of us that could not benefit from understanding and mastering the Stages of Growth concept. The Stages of Growth will identify issues you have faced, are facing and will face and can prepare you to solve current issues/address future issues and, at the same time, align your senior management team and improve communication and morale throughout your firm. I have shared with Stages of Growth with a variety of clients in a variety of industries with Laurie's help. It never fails to deliver."

-Brad Eure, Eure Consulting, LLC

"Laurie Taylor delivered a powerful presentation to our Vail, AZ Chamber of Commerce. The impact of her words resonated with each person in our audience as she identified the 7 Stages of Growth that small businesses navigate as they grow. Being able to put a name to a problem by taking the 27 Challenges exercise had our members excited about knowing exactly where bottlenecks may be, or may arise and how to navigate through them. Regardless of business size, from solo-preneures to major corporations, every member came away thinking differently about themselves and their organizations.

Her insight into how a leader must adapt his/her leadership style to accommodate the different stages of growth is a must know for every business owner or manager. Our members walked away with information they could use immediately to power up to the next stage. Thanks, Laurie!"

-Bekki Harper CEO, Bekki Harper Financial

"Before I tallied the evaluation forms, I knew that you were a hit!

You were able to appeal to a group of business owners and top executives who are diverse in their industries, in their stage of business and in the sizes of their organizations. As I mentioned to you, this market has many one-person businesses, but I also have some of the largest employers in the region as members. You addressed the entire range with great success."

-Ken Keller, STAR Consulting

"Successful business owners will usually figure it out, but often only after it has become a problem. The Navigating the Growth Curve model is uncanny in its ability to accurately predict what is about to happen to business owners, so they can act before it costs them time, emotional energy and money.

As for Laurie Taylor, I gave her a real challenge: give a three-hour pre-sentation to 35 business owners and senior executives. The real challenge? Our group represented every conceivable size and type of company from startups to Fortune 50, from law firms to manufacturing to technology companies. Laurie nailed the presentation giving tremendous value to everyone in the audience. After three hours, these top executives were still in their seats and taking notes. Now that is impressive!"

-Bill McIlwaine, Renaissance Executive Forums

"Laurie's program is credible because she has been through growing a business as a business owner. Her presentation offered succinct tips on how to focus on my business."

-Will Temby, Greater Colorado Springs Chamber of Commerce

"Very informative and extremely eye opening! I really appreciated Laurie's honesty in talking about her own mistakes as a business owner."

-Jon Hicks, Hicks Benefit Group

"Laurie Taylor conducted a 4-hour workshop on the Stages of Growth for 30+ company CEOs, plus several of their management team. She effectively walked the entire group of companies to a clear understanding of this dynamic business model. In addition, she facilitated exercises that allowed the CEOs and their executives to begin to map out plans on how to manage their businesses. She had all parties engaged throughout the workshop.

Prior to being exposed to the Stages of Growth, some of the companies were like bumper cars bouncing around with limited forward motion, focusing on the non-important issues. The Stages are the GPS of business growth in that they provide clarity, focus and direction. Several companies that attended are now implementing the tools and processes that will lead to growth and improved profitability. I recommend Laurie Taylor and the Stages of Growth to any business entity."

-Tony Hutti, Executive Forums

ACKNOWLEDGMENTS

It's been many years since I was in charge of a growing company. However, the memories and the experiences are so vivid it seems like yesterday. I get to share those experiences with business owners every day as I continue to work with small business owners to support their adventures of growing successful businesses.

My real joy today comes from the work I'm doing to support the over 200 business consultants and executive coaches who are now certified to share the 7 Stages of Growth concepts and my programs, The Stages of Growth X-Ray™ and Zeroing in on Your Company's Profit Zone™ with their clients.

Every month, as I work with these advisors, I hear success stories from companies that now embrace the concepts of the 7 Stages of Growth. For instance, a small, but successful manufacturing company that has been in business for over 30 years took their key employees through the X-Ray program. Now each employee is wired into helping the company make and keep more money. The X-Ray program completely changed how those employees viewed the business. The CEO is now surrounded by people who watch expenses and share in the excitement of landing new work.

Or, the CEO of a Stage 6 company who tried to sell the company twice with no results. The reason? The infrastructure wasn't in place and they had ignored some of the critical challenges in previous stages of growth. Once they had gone through the Stages of Growth X-Ray™ program, the company was sold. The new buyer retained the management team because they were doing such a great job running the company.

The reason I am passionate about writing my book series on all seven stages of growth is because no other model goes into so much detail in regards to what a business owner needs to pay attention to as they grow their company. What's even more critical is the fact that this model determines your stage of growth based on how many employees you have. Understanding the impact your people have on the increased complexity of your organization completely changes how a business owner sees their company and their challenges.

I want to acknowledge all of my Growth Curve Specialists, Growth Curve Associates and my Growth Curve Strategists who are helping their clients to be more successful by teaching them the components that make up the 7 Stages of Growth. You know who you are and my appreciation for what you are doing to help business owners succeed grows stronger every day.

I reached out to many of these experienced business growth specialists for input on the chapter on Delegation, and you'll see many of their insights included.

Since July, 2014, my education on the world of business continues to expand because of my work as a mentor with the Southern Arizona SCORE Chapter in Tucson. It's a privilege to listen to bright and enthusiastic entrepreneurs talk about their dreams of owning their own companies. SCORE is a non-profit association dedicated to helping small businesses get off the ground and has been offering free mentoring services and educational classes for over fifty years.

I also want to again give a loud round of applause to Brooke White, my editor, whose skills and insights continue to prove invaluable in pushing me to add critical pieces of information the reader will benefit from. I appreciate her patience and her experience. Connect with her on LinkedIn, https://www.linkedin.com/in/brooke-white-3ba39a18.

My thanks also to Kim Hall, from Inhouse Design Studio, who created the front and back covers and layout for the book. Her creativity helps make these books come alive. Visit her website here: www.inhousedesignstudio.com

I'm always appreciative of James Fischer, for his research on the 7 Stages of Growth and his focus on the small business owner.

If you have ever experienced the benefits of a Master Mind group, you know the value of a group of people who always have your back and who are there to help you grow and learn. I've been a part of a Master Mind group for over eight years, and without their guidance and their friendship, I wouldn't be who I am today. My thanks go out to:

Tom Dearth (www.tomdearth.com)

John Marx (www.copsalive.com)

Terri Norvell (www.theinnerprize.com)

Karen Van Cleve (www.KarenVanCleve.com) and

Karyn Ruth White (www.karenruthwhite.com)

And most of all to my husband, Dave, who is always there to listen and to help and to remind me that I can do whatever I put my mind to.

61150334R00112

Made in the USA
Charleston, SC
17 September 2016